GEO

Lexile: _____

AR/BL: _____

AR Points: _____

Consultant Editors

Michael Chinery · Mary Gibby *PhD* · Esmond Harris *BSs, DipFor, FIFor, Director of the Royal Forestry Society of England, Wales and Northern Ireland* · Peter Olney · Miranda Stevenson, *The Royal Zoological Society of Scotland* · Anthony Wootton and David Carter

Illustrated by

Bob Bampton *(The Garden Studio)* · Joyce Bee · Andrzej Bielecki · Wendy Bramall *(Artist Partners)* · Paul Brooks *(John Martin Artists)* · Mark Burgess · Martin Camm · Frankie Coventry *(Artist Partners)* · Michelle Emblem *(Middletons)* · Denise Finney · Sarah Fox-Davies · Judy Friedlander · Sheila Galbraith · Victoria Goaman · David Hurrell *(Middletons)* · Roy Hutchison *(Middletons)* · Elaine Keenan · Richard Lewington *(The Garden Studio)* · Mick Loates *(The Garden Studio)* · Andy Martin · Malcolm McGregor · Dee McLean *(Linden Artists)* · David More *(Linden Artists)* · Dee Morgan · Robert Morton *(Linden Artists)* · Liz Pepperell *(The Garden Studio)* · Cynthia Pow *(Middletons)* · Coral Sealey · Chris Shields *(Wilcock Riley)* · John Sibbick *(John Martin Artists)* · Ralph Stobart · John Thompson-Steinkrauss *(John Martin Artists)* · Sally Voke *(Middletons)* · James Woods *(Middletons)* · David Wright *(Jillian Burgess)*

Designed by

David Bennett · Anne Sharples · Andrzej Bielecki

Language Consultants

Gillian Ghate · Betty Root

First published in 1990 by Usborne Publishing Ltd, Usborne House, 83-85 Saffron Hill, London EC1N 8RT, England.

© 1990 by Usborne Publishing Ltd.

The name Usborne and the device 🐝 are Trade Marks of Usborne Publishing Ltd.

Printed in Belgium

THE USBORNE COMPLETE FIRST BOOK OF NATURE

BIRDS

Games

2. Watch the bird fly

Hold the
Bird pages
like this.

1. Hunt the Grasshopper

Some birds eat
Grasshoppers. Can you
find 13 more Grasshoppers
in the Bird pages?

Watch the top right hand corner
and flick the pages over fast.

← watch here

Looking at birds

A bird is like
an aeroplane.

Its shape helps it to
move fast through the air.

A bird is like
a bat.

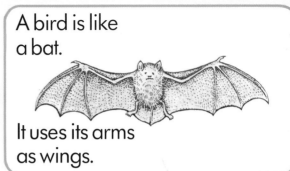

It uses its arms
as wings.

Swallow

A bird is like
a weightlifter.
It has strong arm
and chest muscles.

A bird is like
a balloon.
It has lots of air
inside its body.

Birds are the only
animals in the world
that have feathers.

Birds have three kinds of feathers.

1. Down feathers.
They help keep the bird warm.

2. Body feathers.
They cover the body.

3. Flight feathers.
They help the bird to fly.

Greylag goose

Down feathers are under the body feathers.

body feathers

flight feathers

Birds grow a new set of feathers every year.

A goose cannot fly while its new flight feathers are growing.

baby goose

down feathers

Baby birds have down feathers to help keep them warm.

3

Bee-eater

Hummingbird

Wood Warbler

Taking off and flying

Blue Tit

When birds want to take off, they leap into the air and flap their wings as fast as they can.

Mute Swan

Some birds are too heavy to leap into the air. Before they can take off they have to run along flapping their wings.

Mallard

Tawny Owl

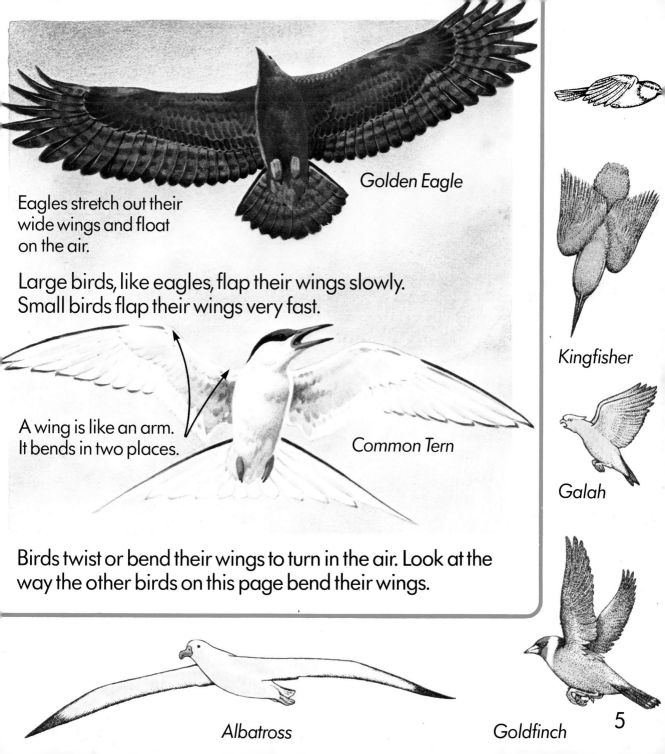

Golden Eagle

Eagles stretch out their wide wings and float on the air.

Large birds, like eagles, flap their wings slowly. Small birds flap their wings very fast.

A wing is like an arm. It bends in two places.

Common Tern

Kingfisher

Galah

Birds twist or bend their wings to turn in the air. Look at the way the other birds on this page bend their wings.

Albatross

Goldfinch

5

Why do birds fly?

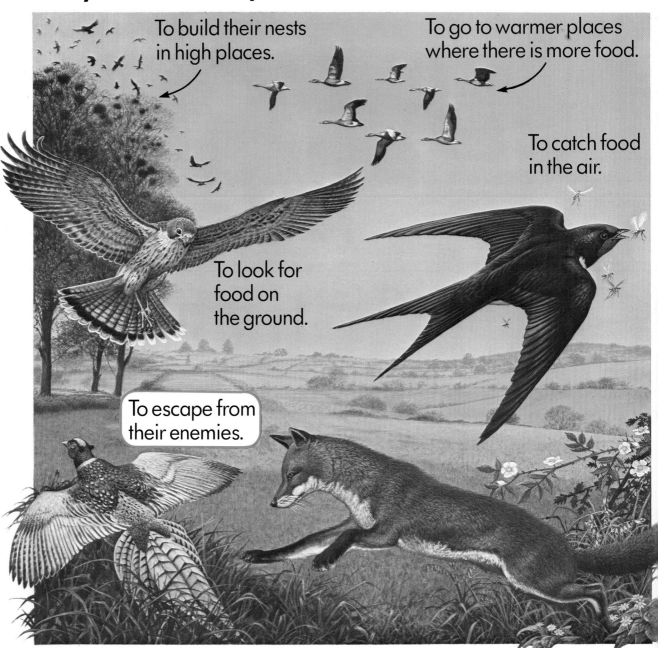

To build their nests in high places.

To go to warmer places where there is more food.

To catch food in the air.

To look for food on the ground.

To escape from their enemies.

Why do birds land?

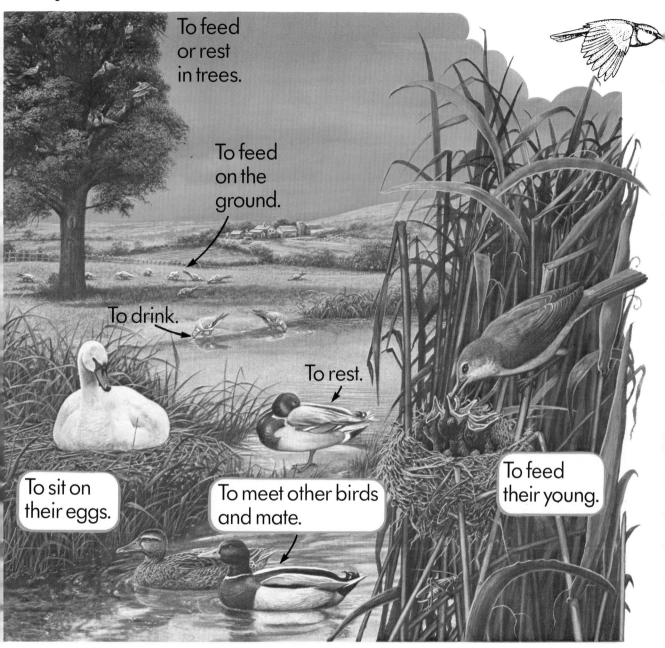

To feed or rest in trees.

To feed on the ground.

To drink.

To rest.

To sit on their eggs.

To meet other birds and mate.

To feed their young.

Legs and feet

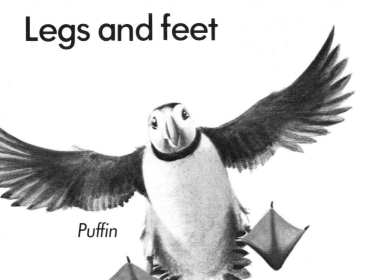

Puffin

A bird puts out its feet to land. It also spreads out its tail and wings to slow down.

Birds walk on their toes. They can run or hop along the ground.

A bird's leg bends here.

Marabou Stork

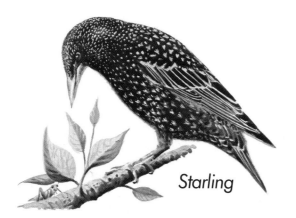

Starling

This bird rests on branches. When it bends its legs, its toes lock on to the branch.

Some birds rest on the ground. Storks often sit like this when they rest

Birds often stand on one leg.
They tuck the other leg
under their feathers
to keep it warm.

Coot

Mallard

Water birds have skin between their toes. The skin helps them to use their feet as paddles and to walk on mud without sinking in.

Snowy Owl

The feathers on
its feet help it
to walk on the snow
without sinking in.

The Snowy Owl has claws like daggers. It kills with its feet.
Its feet are covered with feathers to keep them warm.

Beaks and feeding

Birds have no teeth so they cannot chew food. They swallow food whole and then grind it up in their stomachs.

Kookaburra

Black Kite

This bird uses its hooked beak to tear up its food.

strainer

Shoveler

This duck uses its beak as a strainer. It collects tiny plants and animals from the top of the water.

Magpie

Pelicans

pouch

Crossbill

A Pelican uses its huge beak to scoop fish from the water. Its beak can hold more food than its stomach.

10

Hummingbird

Rosella

Birds have different kinds of beaks because they eat different kinds of food. These seashore birds can feed close together because they eat different animals.

Godwits poke their beaks a short way into the mud to catch small animals.

Curlews have very long beaks. They eat animals that live deep in the mud.

Woodpecker

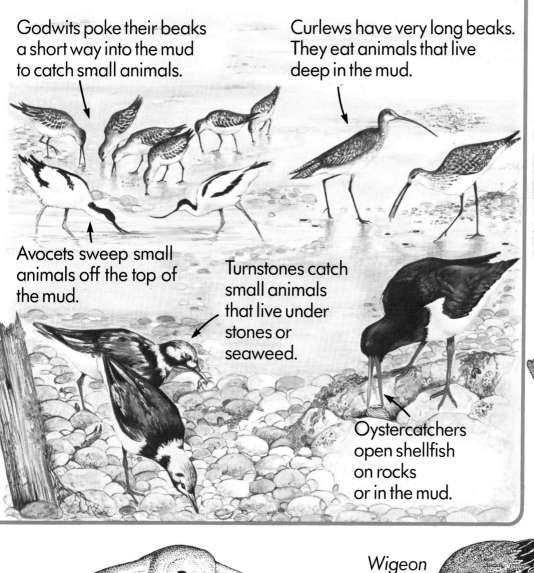

Avocets sweep small animals off the top of the mud.

Turnstones catch small animals that live under stones or seaweed.

Oystercatchers open shellfish on rocks or in the mud.

Splendid Wren

Wigeon

Barn Owl

11

Colours

Many birds match the colour of the leaves and branches of the trees they rest in. This helps them to hide from their enemies.

There are seven birds in this picture.
Can you see them all?

Frogmouth

When birds are sitting on eggs, they need to be hidden. This female Nightjar is sitting on her eggs. She is hard to see.

The Australian Frogmouth sleeps all day in a tree. It sits very still with its head up. It looks just like a broken branch.

Birds may use their colours to recognize each other.

Oystercatchers live together in big groups. If some of the birds fly off
to a new feeding place, the others soon follow. They recognize each other
by their colours and the calls that they make.

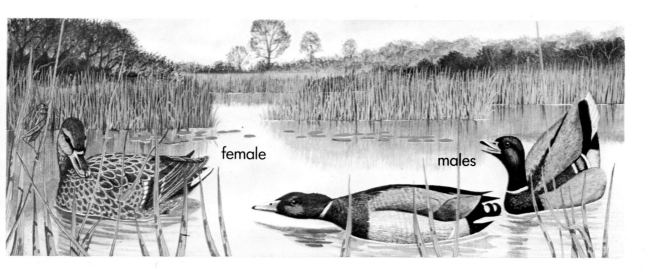

female

males

Male and female Mallards are different colours. Male Mallards are most colourful
in the breeding season. They show off their bright colours in a special dance.
This attracts a female for mating.

13

Song and dance

Birds sing most of all in the breeding season.

Male Blackbirds sing to attract female Blackbirds.

female Blackbird

Male Blackbirds also sing to tell other male Blackbirds "This is where I live so keep away".

Tawny Owls

Owls find each other in the dark by calling.

The male Pigeon has to dance in front of the female before he can mate with her. He turns in circles and "coos" loudly all the time.

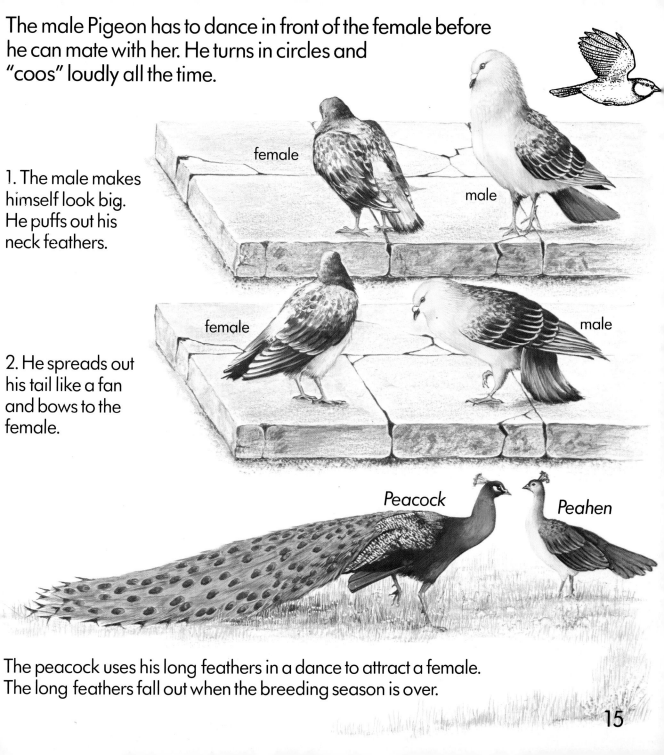

1. The male makes himself look big. He puffs out his neck feathers.

female

male

2. He spreads out his tail like a fan and bows to the female.

female

male

Peacock

Peahen

The peacock uses his long feathers in a dance to attract a female. The long feathers fall out when the breeding season is over.

Eggs and nests

Soon after a female bird has mated, she lays her eggs. If she kept all her eggs inside her until they were ready to hatch, she would probably be too heavy to fly.

Guillemot eggs

Oystercatcher eggs

The female Common Tern lays her eggs on the ground. A baby Tern grows inside each egg.

The eggs match the colour of the ground around them. It is hard for enemies to see them.

When baby Terns hatch, they are covered with down. The down helps keep them warm.

If an enemy is about, the baby Terns crouch down so they are difficult to see.

Rook eggs

Eider Duc[k] eggs

Most birds build nests. The nest hides the eggs and baby birds from enemies. It helps to keep them warm. Birds also sit on their eggs to keep them warm. If the eggs get cold, the baby birds inside them will die.

Song Thrushes

Rock Warbler nest

The male Thrush feeds the female. She sits on the eggs for two weeks.

Baby birds that hatch in nests are naked and blind. Their parents look after them.

Hummingbird eggs

Kingfisher nest

Golden Oriole eggs

17

Growing up

Song Thrush

Thrushes collect food from their home area near the nest.

Baby Thrushes stay in the nest for two weeks until most of their feathers have grown.

Baby birds are always hungry. When their parents land on the nest, the baby birds open their beaks wide and call loudly. The bright colours inside their beaks make their parents feed them.

Baby Herring Gulls peck the red spot to get a meal.

Older Herring Gulls peck at the top of the beak.

Herring Gulls may have to fly far away to collect food for their babies. They swallow the food that they collect. When they get back, they cough up the food for the babies to eat.

18

Baby geese may watch their parents to find out what to eat.

They may sit on their mother's back if they are cold or tired.

A short time after they hatch, baby geese can swim. They will go into the water to escape from enemies.

Young geese take about six weeks to grow all their feathers.
They can now fly, but they may practise twisting and turning in the air.
They may also practise taking off and landing.

Resting and preening

At night most birds find a safe place to rest. They do not like flying at night because they cannot see well in the dark.

Hundreds of Starlings often fly to the same place every evening. They all rest together for the night.

Some birds tuck their beaks under their wings when they sleep. They fluff out their feathers to keep themselves warm.

Sparrows

Lots of Wrens may sleep together to keep warm.

Birds don't fall out of trees when they sleep. This is because when they bend their legs, their toes lock on to the branch.

All birds clean and tidy up their feathers.
This is called preening. Most birds also spread oil
on their feathers to keep them in good condition.

Birds squeeze oil
out of a gland
just above the tail.

Herring Gulls

oil gland

Lovebirds

Some birds preen each other.

Song Thrush

Some birds have a bath.

Birds that do not fly

The Ostrich is the largest bird in the world. It is too heavy to fly and it has only small wing feathers. The Ostrich cannot fly away from enemies, but it can look after itself in other ways.

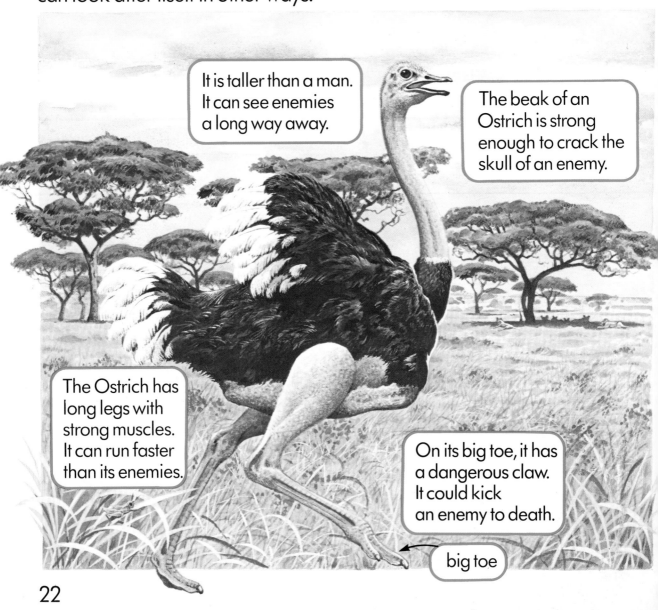

It is taller than a man. It can see enemies a long way away.

The beak of an Ostrich is strong enough to crack the skull of an enemy.

The Ostrich has long legs with strong muscles. It can run faster than its enemies.

On its big toe, it has a dangerous claw. It could kick an enemy to death.

big toe

Penguins do not fly with their wings. Do you know how they use them?

Penguins use their wings as flippers. They can swim very fast on top of the water or under the water.

Penguins use their wings to help them balance.

These Penguins are hunting for fish.

Penguins use their wings and their beaks when they quarrel.

Penguins can jump out of the sea.

Rockhopper Penguins

23

Picture puzzle

There are 13 birds hidden in this picture.
Can you find them all?

TREES

Games

1. Hunt the Nut Weevil

Nut Weevils live on trees. Can you find 10 more Nut Weevils in the Tree pages ?

2. Watch the leaf bud open

Hold the Tree pages like this.

Watch the top right hand corner and flick the pages over fast.

watch here

Amazing facts about trees

Trees are the largest plants in the world. They also live the longest.

On a warm day in spring, a large tree like this takes up 250 gallons of water from the soil. The water would fill five baths.

Trees cover about one third of the earth's surface.

Sometimes, the roots of a tree spread wider than its branches.

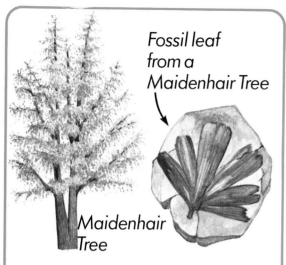

Fossil leaf from a Maidenhair Tree

Maidenhair Tree

Maidenhair trees today look almost the same as ones that grew 200 million years ago.

Bristlecone Pine Tree

This tree has been alive for 4,900 years.
It grows in America.

People say that this tree has enough wood to make all these bungalows. It is the biggest tree in the world. It is 83 metres tall and 24 metres round the trunk.

This Sierra Redwood tree grows in California, in North America.

Trees in the countryside

This picture shows you some of the places where trees grow. Some of them grow naturally and some are planted by people.

This is a windy hillside. The branches of the trees grow bent over because of the wind.

Trees in a wood grow close together. They have thin trunks and not very many lower branches.

People sometimes plant trees around their houses to protect them from wind and frost.

A tree growing on its own has spreading branches.

Some trees grow near water.

Few trees can grow here. It is too cold and windy.

Foresters plant pine and spruce trees in straight lines. These trees grow very quickly.

Trees are sometimes planted along roads to give shade.

Every few years, some of the trees are cut down. This gives the stronger trees more room to grow.

Trees often mark the edges of fields. They also stop the soil blowing away.

Under the ground

Roots help a tree in many ways. They take up water and minerals from the soil. A tree needs these to grow. They hold the tree in place and they also hold the soil together. On steep ground, they help stop the soil from washing away in the rain.

Oak Tree

These roots are very strong and woody. They help to hold the tree firmly in the ground and stop it from blowing over.

Worm

This grub eats soft, new roots.

The roots grow a little thicker each year.

Each tree has a main root. This is called the tap root. It grows deep and straight into the ground.

If a root comes to a stone, it grows around it.

30

Dead leaves fall to the ground. Worms pull them into the soil. The dead leaves contain minerals, which the roots will use again.

Some fungi grow on roots. They help the tree to feed.

Side roots grow near the surface of the soil, where there is air and water.

Feeding roots grow from the side roots. They take in water and minerals through their tips. After a few years they die. New roots grow and find fresh soil.

Cockchafer grub

Root tips grow all the time. They push through the soil. They are covered with hairs. These hairs take in water and minerals.

All roots grow towards water in the soil.

31

How a twig grows

This is how a Beech twig grows in one year.

This is the leading bud. It is covered with scales that protect it. The new stem and leaves are inside the scales.

These are side buds.

1. Winter

The new stem grows and the leaves unfold. The scales are pushed apart.

The side buds grow into side shoots.

The new leaves are soft and pale.

2. Spring

3. Summer

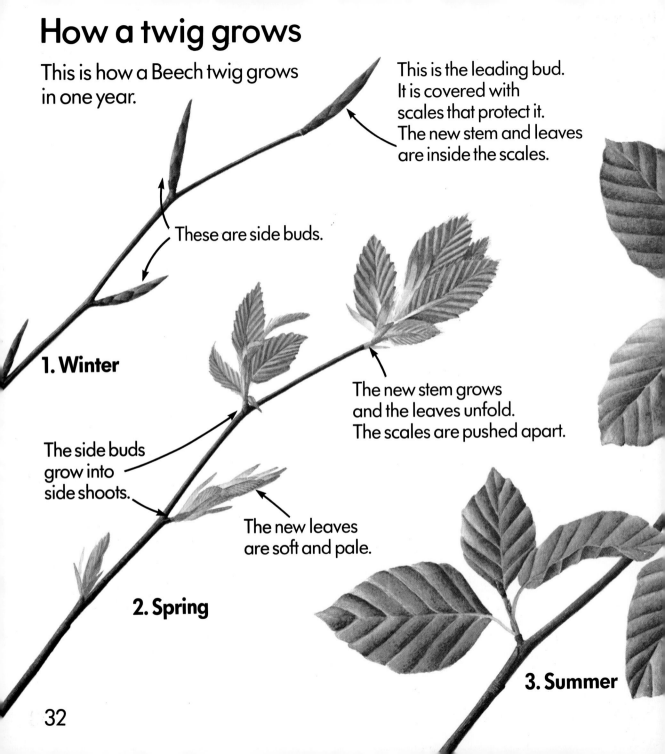

By summer, the stems are stiff and the leaves are dark green and shiny.

When the twig stops growing, it makes a new leading bud. Next spring, this bud will grow into a new shoot.

The leaves turn brown before they fall off.

Towards the end of summer, a new bud is made just above each leaf stalk. Next year, this bud will grow into a new side shoot.

This is where the leading bud was in the winter. The bud scales have left a scar. It is called a girdle scar. If you count the girdle scars on a twig, you can find out how old the twig is. This twig is two years old.

4. Autumn

33

Tree stumps

This is the inside of a healthy tree stump.

Most of the inside is sapwood. This carries water and minerals up from the roots to the leaves.

A very thin layer under the bark makes a new ring of sapwood every year.

In the middle is the heartwood. It is old, dead sapwood. It is very hard and strong.

Bark stops the tree from drying out and protects it from insects and disease. Bark cannot stretch. It splits or peels as the wood inside grows. New bark grows underneath.

This is how a tree may die.

spores

Fungus spores in the air get into a wound in the tree.

The fungus spreads inside the trunk. The heartwood rots.

The heartwood in this tree is rotten.

Once the tree gets weak inside, it falls over in a storm.

When a tree dies, the bark becomes loose.
Animals and plants can get under the bark.
Many of them feed on the rotting wood.

Bracket Fungi grow
on the trunk and feed
on the rotting wood.

Slugs eat dead leaves and fungi.
In dry weather they hide in
cracks under the bark.

Longhorn Beetle

Scarlet
Cup Fungi

Centipedes live under the
bark. They come out at night
to hunt for small insects.

Bark Beetles and their
grubs make long
tunnels under
the bark.

Woodlice hide in damp
places under the bark.
They feed on rotting wood.

Millipedes live on the ground.
They feed on dead leaves.

5

Deciduous tree leaves

Many trees are deciduous. This means that they lose their leaves in autumn. Most deciduous trees have soft, flat leaves.

Lime trees lose their leaves in autumn.

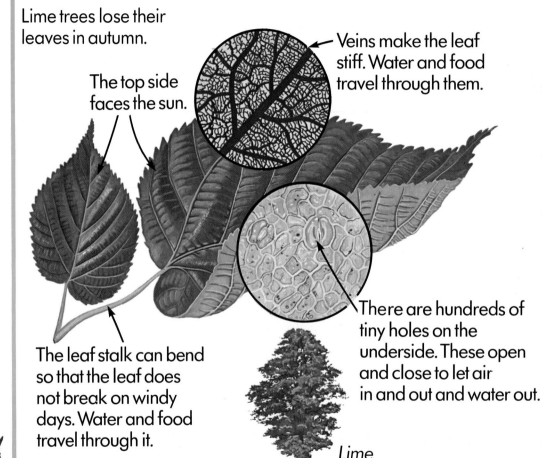

Veins make the leaf stiff. Water and food travel through them.

The top side faces the sun.

There are hundreds of tiny holes on the underside. These open and close to let air in and out and water out.

The leaf stalk can bend so that the leaf does not break on windy days. Water and food travel through it.

Rowan

Oak

Lime

Sycamore

Quaking Aspen

Horse Chestnut

Evergreen tree leaves

Other trees are called evergreens.
They keep their leaves all winter.
Most evergreens have tough, waxy leaves.

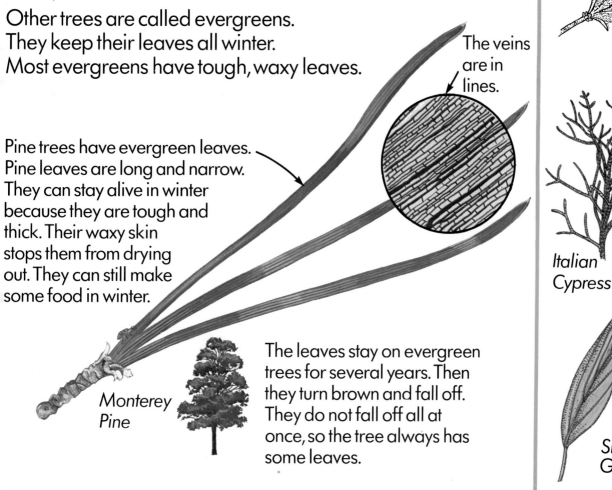

The veins are in lines.

Pine trees have evergreen leaves.
Pine leaves are long and narrow.
They can stay alive in winter
because they are tough and
thick. Their waxy skin
stops them from drying
out. They can still make
some food in winter.

Monterey Pine

The leaves stay on evergreen
trees for several years. Then
they turn brown and fall off.
They do not fall off all at
once, so the tree always has
some leaves.

Italian Cypress

Snow Gum

Leaves are many different shapes, but they all do the same
work. Turn over the page to see what they do.

Norway Spruce

Juniper

Evergreen Oak

Scots Pine

What leaves do

A tree breathes and feeds with its leaves.
Follow the numbers to see how a tree makes its food.

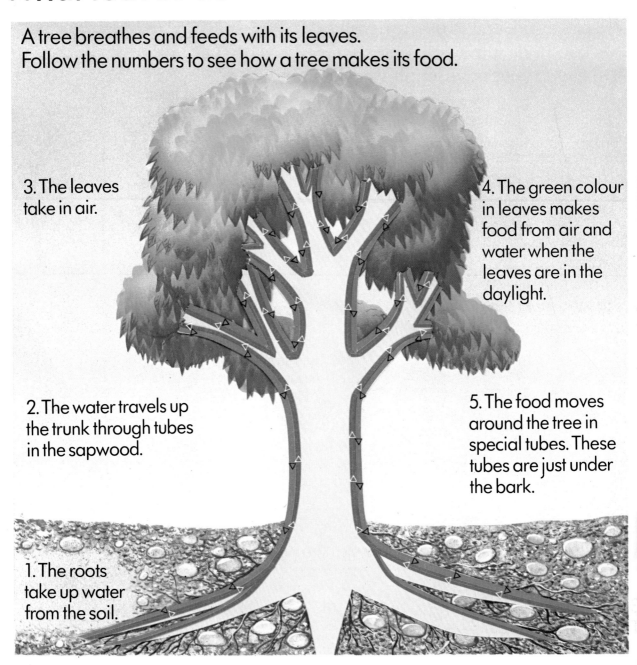

3. The leaves take in air.

4. The green colour in leaves makes food from air and water when the leaves are in the daylight.

2. The water travels up the trunk through tubes in the sapwood.

5. The food moves around the tree in special tubes. These tubes are just under the bark.

1. The roots take up water from the soil.

Why do deciduous trees lose their leaves in autumn?

Silver Maple

The corky layer forms here.

1. In autumn, it is not warm enough for leaves to make much food. Also, wind and cold weather would damage soft leaves.

2. A corky layer grows across the leaf stalk. Water cannot get to the leaf any more. The leaf changes colour.

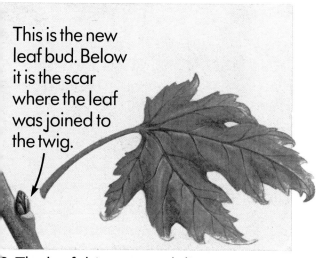

This is the new leaf bud. Below it is the scar where the leaf was joined to the twig.

3. The leaf dries out and dies. The wind blows it off the tree.

4. All the leaves fall off. The tree rests until spring.

Tree flowers

All trees have flowers. Flowers have stamens, which hold pollen, and a pistil, which holds ovules. Pollen that lands on the top of the pistil grows down to join with the ovules. This is called fertilization. Fertilized ovules grow into seeds.

1. The petals and sweet scent attract insects. The insects feed on a sweet liquid inside the flower. This is called nectar.

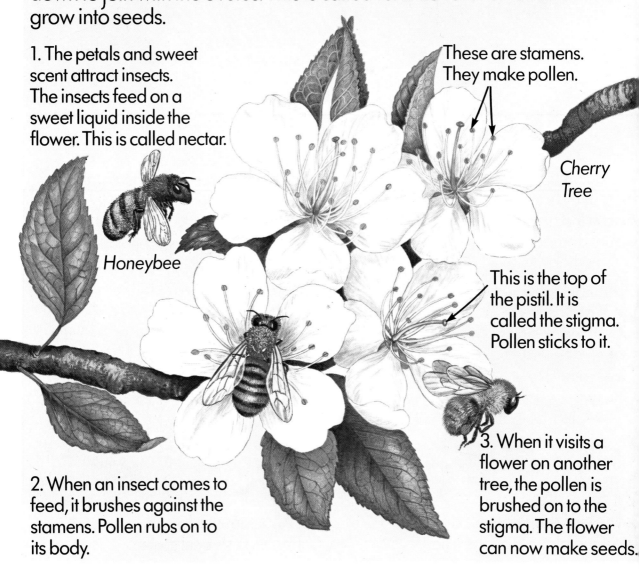

These are stamens. They make pollen.

Cherry Tree

Honeybee

This is the top of the pistil. It is called the stigma. Pollen sticks to it.

2. When an insect comes to feed, it brushes against the stamens. Pollen rubs on to its body.

3. When it visits a flower on another tree, the pollen is brushed on to the stigma. The flower can now make seeds.

40

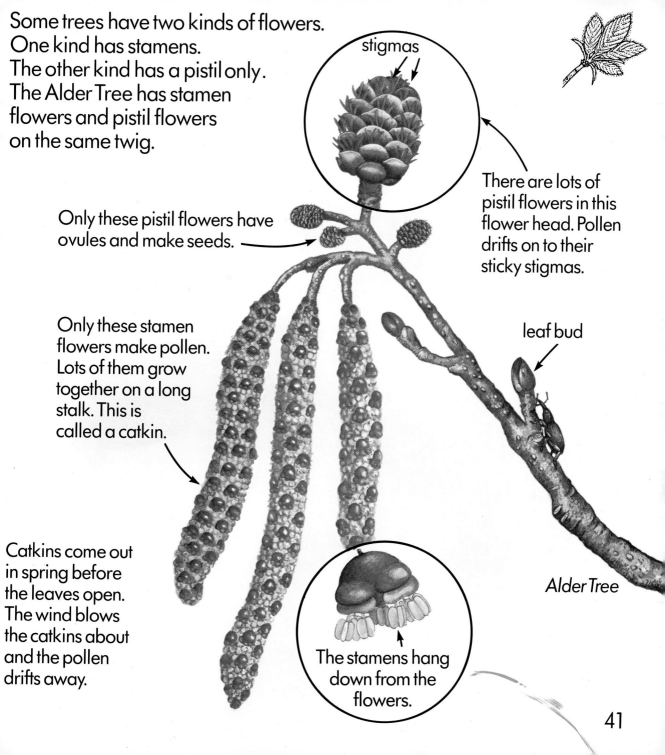

Some trees have two kinds of flowers.
One kind has stamens.
The other kind has a pistil only.
The Alder Tree has stamen
flowers and pistil flowers
on the same twig.

stigmas

There are lots of
pistil flowers in this
flower head. Pollen
drifts on to their
sticky stigmas.

Only these pistil flowers have
ovules and make seeds.

leaf bud

Only these stamen
flowers make pollen.
Lots of them grow
together on a long
stalk. This is
called a catkin.

Catkins come out
in spring before
the leaves open.
The wind blows
the catkins about
and the pollen
drifts away.

Alder Tree

The stamens hang
down from the
flowers.

41

Fruits and seeds

The fertilized ovules grow into seeds. Fruits grow to hold and protect them.

Sitka Spruce

Lime

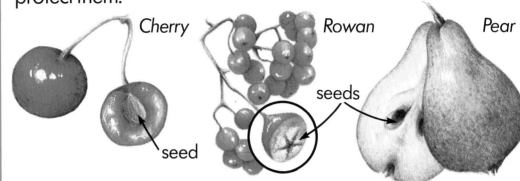

Cherry

seed

Rowan

seeds

Pear

seeds

These fruits are soft and juicy. Birds and animals eat them. Some have only one seed inside, others have lots.

Horse Chestnut

seed

Willow

seed

Hornbeam

Seed is in here

wing

This fruit is spiky. It protects the seed inside.

This fruit is made of lots of seeds with feathery tops.

This fruit is hard and dry. It has a leafy wing.

Plane

Beech

Birch

Hazel

Many evergreen trees have fruits called cones. The flowers that grow at the tips of new shoots grow into cones. Sometimes this takes two years.

Pine flowers are made up of soft scales. Each scale has two ovules inside. When pollen lands on the ovules they start to change into seeds. The scales close up to protect the seeds.

A Pine flower cut in half

ovules

Pine flower

This cone is a year old. The seeds inside are not ripe yet. The scales are hard and tightly shut.

Yew

Juniper

This cone is two years old. It is large and woody. The seeds inside are ripe. On a dry day, the scales open and the seeds fall out.

Scots Pine

seeds

Crab Apple

Mulberry

Sweet Chestnut

Black Locust

43

How seeds are moved

When the seeds in the fruits are ripe, the wind or animals may move them away from the tree. There is not enough light under the parent tree for the seedlings to grow well.

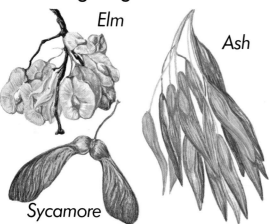

Elm

Ash

Sycamore

Fruits with wings spin away from the tree.

Plane

White Poplar

Some fruits are very light. They have tiny hairs that help them float away in the wind.

acorn

Oak Tree

Squirrels carry acorns away from Oak Trees and bury them. Birds feed on acorns and drop some. A few of the acorns grow into trees.

Birds carry the fruits and seeds away from these trees. They eat the fruits and drop the seeds.

Fieldfare

Holly

Blackthorn

Dogwood

Elder

Hawthorn

Waxwing

Alder cone

seeds

Alder Trees grow near water. Their seeds drop in the water and float away. Some seeds will be washed up on a damp river bank. They may grow into new trees.

45

Life on a tree

Keep a record book about a tree.
See how many insects live on the leaves or rest on the bark.
Watch how many birds visit it. Notice if any plants grow on it.

JUNE

I found a weevil on a leaf.

When I touched it, it folded its legs.

JUNE

I saw these willow fruits.

Herald Moth caterpillar

Some caterpillars are difficult to spot. Search carefully for them.

Dragonfly

Flying insects sometimes rest on the leaves in summer.

Willow fruits

Look for Willow fruits in spring and summer.

Poplar Hawk Moth

Some moths rest on the trunk in the day. They fly at night.

White Willow

Leaf Beetle

Look for beetles on the leaves and flowers.

Birds often visit trees to nest or sleep. Some search for seeds or insects.

Red Underwing Moth

These animals live on Willow trees. Willow trees often grow in wet places.

Picture puzzle

People eat many things that grow on trees. They make many things from the wood. There are at least 20 things in this picture that come from trees. How many can you find?

FLOWERS

Games

1. Hunt the Bumblebee

Bumblebees visit flowers. Can you find 20 more Bumblebees in the Flower pages?

2. Watch the flower open

Hold the Flower pages like this.

Watch the top right hand corner and flick the pages over fast.

watch here

Looking at Buttercup flowers

If you look closely at a flower, you will see that it is made of lots of different parts.

sepal

1. A bud is a baby flower wrapped up in sepals. The sepals protect the flower parts inside.

petal

sepal

open flower

petal

sepal

opening flower

3. If you look under a Buttercup flower you can see the five sepals.

2. As the petals grow, the sepals are pushed apart.

stamens   pistil

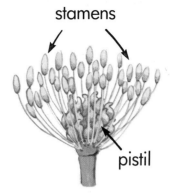

stamens

pistil

Inside the ring of petals are more flower parts. The green parts in the centre are called the pistil. Around it are stamens.

If you pull off the petals and sepals, you can see all the parts inside.

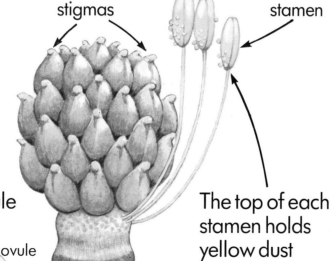

stigmas   stamen

Each part of the pistil has a sticky top called a stigma.

There is a tiny ovule inside each part of the pistil. It will grow into a seed.

ovule

The top of each stamen holds yellow dust called pollen.

51

Looking at flower parts

Flower parts can be different shapes and sizes and different colours. You will have to look closely at each flower to see which part is which.

Bindweed

Lily

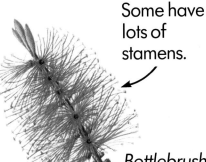

Some flowers have petals joined together.

Harebell

Some have petals of different shapes and sizes. →

Violet

Pink

Some have lots of stamens.

Bottlebrush

Some have brightly coloured sepals and brightly coloured petals.

Fuchsia

Vetch

Columbine

Some flowers have a pistil with only one stigma.

Daffodil

Crocus

Some have a pistil with more than one stigma.

Cranesbill

An Aster flower is made of lots of tiny flowers.

An Aster has tiny flowers on the outside with one long petal.

If you pull an Aster to bits, you can see the tiny yellow flowers on the inside.

The Bumblebee is somewhere on this page. Do you know why he visits flowers? The answer is on the next page.

Daisy

Dandelion

Dahlia

53

The visitors

Cranesbill

Flowers have many visitors. They are usually insects, such as bees. The Bumblebee visits flowers to drink a sweet liquid called nectar. Sometimes the visitors eat some of the pollen.

Yellow Flag

Visitors to this flower need long tongues to reach down to the nectar.

Many flowers have guide-lines or dots that point the way to the nectar.

Nectar is in here.

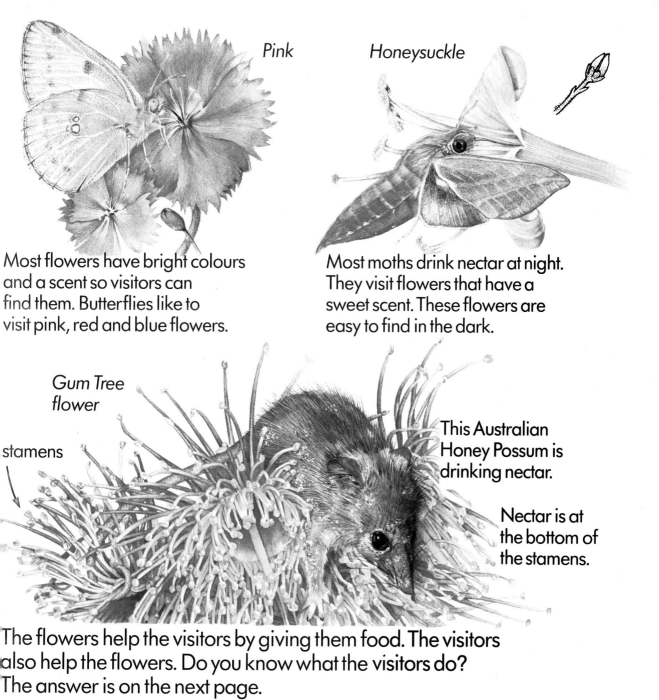

Pink

Honeysuckle

Most flowers have bright colours and a scent so visitors can find them. Butterflies like to visit pink, red and blue flowers.

Most moths drink nectar at night. They visit flowers that have a sweet scent. These flowers are easy to find in the dark.

Gum Tree flower

stamens

This Australian Honey Possum is drinking nectar.

Nectar is at the bottom of the stamens.

The flowers help the visitors by giving them food. The visitors also help the flowers. Do you know what the visitors do? The answer is on the next page.

Why flowers need visitors

Visitors help plants by moving pollen from flower to flower.

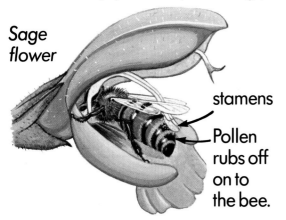

Sage flower

stamens

Pollen rubs off on to the bee.

pollen

1. As a bee collects nectar from a flower, its body gets covered with pollen.

2. It flies to another Sage flower. It has pollen from the first flower on its back.

stigma

stamens

3. As it lands, the pollen on the bee's body rubs on to the stigma of the flower.

4. The bee goes into the flower. New pollen from the stamens rubs on to its back.

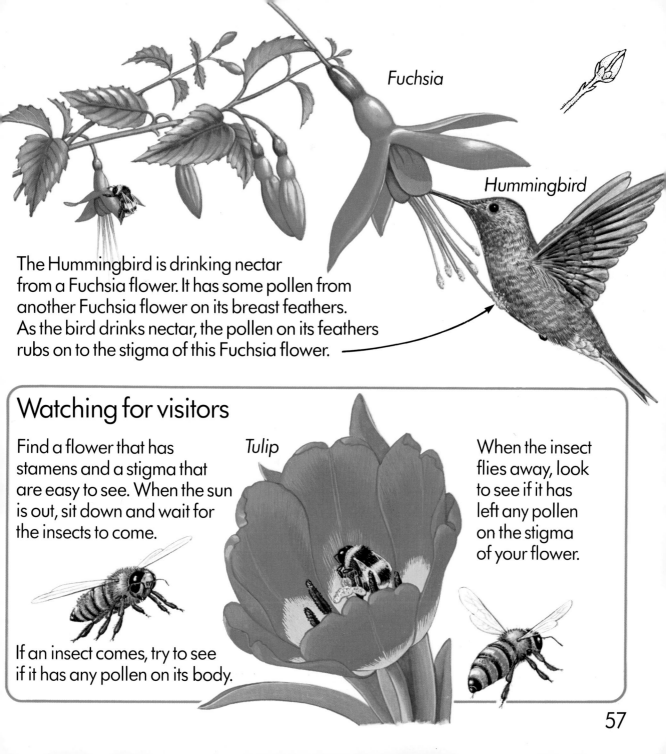

Fuchsia

Hummingbird

The Hummingbird is drinking nectar from a Fuchsia flower. It has some pollen from another Fuchsia flower on its breast feathers. As the bird drinks nectar, the pollen on its feathers rubs on to the stigma of this Fuchsia flower.

Watching for visitors

Find a flower that has stamens and a stigma that are easy to see. When the sun is out, sit down and wait for the insects to come.

Tulip

When the insect flies away, look to see if it has left any pollen on the stigma of your flower.

If an insect comes, try to see if it has any pollen on its body.

How the wind helps flowers

The flowers on this page do not need visitors to move their pollen. The wind blows their pollen from flower to flower.

Plantain flowers

False Oat Grass flowers

Wood-Rush flowers

These flowers have no scent or coloured petals to attract visitors.

Plantain

They have lots of stamens with lots of pollen. The wind blows it away.

In spring you may see clouds of pollen blowing off grass flowers. Most of this pollen will be wasted, but some will stick on to the stigmas of the grass flowers.

Rye flowers

All trees have flowers. Many trees use the wind to move their pollen.

The Walnut Tree has two kinds of flowers. One kind of flower has a large pistil. The other kind of flower is made of lots of stamens.

stigmas

pistil

stamens

pistil flower

3. If pollen from stamen flowers blows past a pistil flower, it will stick to the stigmas.

1. Lots of stamen flowers grow together on a stalk. Each stalk is called a catkin.

2. The wind blows the pollen off the catkin. Some of the pollen may land on a pistil flower.

pistil flower

Hazel Tree flowers

stamen flowers

pistil flowers

stamen flowers

Larch Tree flowers

59

What happens to the pollen

stigma

stamen

pistil

1. A bee has left pollen on this stigma. The pollen came from another Poppy flower.

2. Each grain of pollen grows a tube down inside the pistil.
There are ovules inside the pistil.

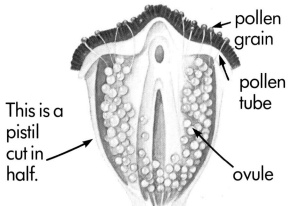

pollen grain

pollen tube

This is a pistil cut in half.

ovule

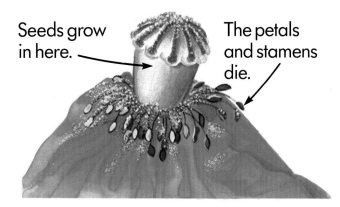

Seeds grow in here.

The petals and stamens die.

3. When a tube reaches an ovule, the inside of the pollen grain moves out of the tube and joins with the ovule.

4. The ovules in the pistil have been fertilized by the pollen.
The fertilized ovules will grow into Poppy seeds.

60

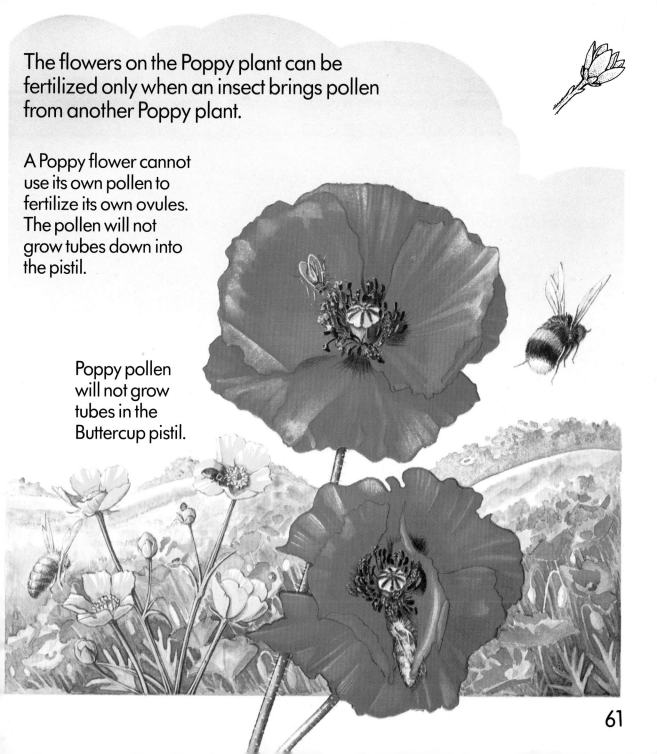

The flowers on the Poppy plant can be fertilized only when an insect brings pollen from another Poppy plant.

A Poppy flower cannot use its own pollen to fertilize its own ovules. The pollen will not grow tubes down into the pistil.

Poppy pollen will not grow tubes in the Buttercup pistil.

More about pollen

Many flowers are like the Poppy. They do not use their own pollen to fertilize themselves. Pollen must be brought from another flower of the same kind by visitors or by the wind.

A single flower of the Yellow Mountain Saxifrage can never fertilize itself because the stamens die before the stigmas are ripe.

stamens

no stigmas

The flowers on this plant are less than a week old. Only the stamens are ripe.

stigmas

old stamen

The flowers on this plant are more than eleven days old. The stigmas are ripe. The stamens are dead.

The pollen of this Bee Orchid is moved only by male Eucera Bees. But if no Eucera Bees visit the Orchid it will use its own pollen to fertilize itself.

1. This Bee Orchid looks and smells like a female Eucera Bee. This is how the Orchid attracts male Eucera Bees.

Two sacs of pollen.

2. If a male Bee lands on a flower, the two pollen sacs stick on to his head.

3. This is another male Eucera Bee. He has pollen on his head from another Bee Orchid.

Stigma is in here.

4. As he lands on this flower, the pollen will stick on to the stigma and fertilize the flower.

If no Bees visit this Bee Orchid, it will fertilize itself.

This is how the Bee Orchid fertilizes itself.

The stamens bend over.

The Pollen sacs touch the stigma.

63

How seeds leave the plant

1. The ovules in this Poppy pistil have been fertilized. They are growing into seeds.

2. The pistil swells. It is now a fruit with seeds inside it.

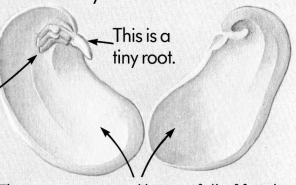

3. Holes open in the top. When the wind blows the fruit, the seeds fall out.

Looking inside a seed

This is a bean seed. It has a thick skin to protect the parts inside.

If you split open a bean seed, this is what you will see inside.

This is a tiny root.

This tiny shoot will grow into a new plant.

These are two seed leaves full of food. The shoot will use this food when it grows.

When the seeds in the fruits are ripe, the wind
or animals may move them away from the plant.

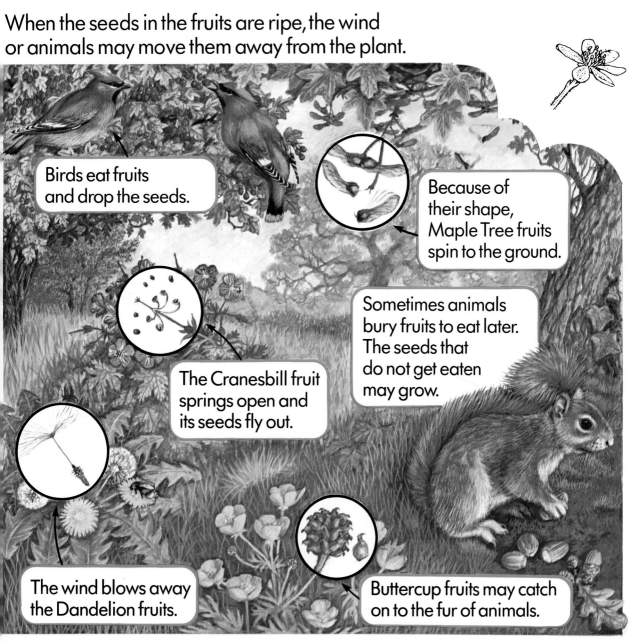

Birds eat fruits
and drop the seeds.

Because of
their shape,
Maple Tree fruits
spin to the ground.

Sometimes animals
bury fruits to eat later.
The seeds that
do not get eaten
may grow.

The Cranesbill fruit
springs open and
its seeds fly out.

The wind blows away
the Dandelion fruits.

Buttercup fruits may catch
on to the fur of animals.

Plants make lots of seeds but only a few of the seeds will grow into new
plants. The others die or get eaten.

How a seed grows

1. Autumn
A bird drops a Sunflower seed by accident.

2. Winter
The seed falls to the ground and gets covered over.

3. Spring
Rain makes the seed swell. A root grows down into the soil.

6. Late spring
The Sunflower plant grows a flower bud. The plant is now taller than a person.

bud

7. Summer
The buds open.

Nasturtium

Pea

66

Oak acorn

Sycamore

4. Spring

The shoot grows towards the light.

Seed leaves

5. Spring

The baby plant uses the food in the seed leaves to grow.

Proper leaves start to grow. They will make food.

The root takes water and minerals from the soil.

Bees bring pollen from other Sunflowers.

8. Autumn

The flowers have been fertilized.

A bird eats the seeds.

Broad Bean

Acacia

Sweet Pea

Maize

How flowers and insects work together

Flowers make most nectar and scent when their pistil or stamens are ripe because this is when they need to attract visitors.

Bees visit these Cherry flowers in the morning. This is when the flowers have most nectar.

New Honeysuckle flowers open in the evening. This is when moths visit them.

The flowers make lots of scent in the evening, but only a little scent in the day.

Bees visit these Apple flowers in the afternoon. This is when the flowers have most nectar.

Many plants take several weeks to open all their flowers. Bees come back to these plants day after day until all the flowers are over.

The Willowherb takes about a month to open all its flowers. The first flowers to open are at the bottom of the stem. The last flowers to open are at the top of the stem.

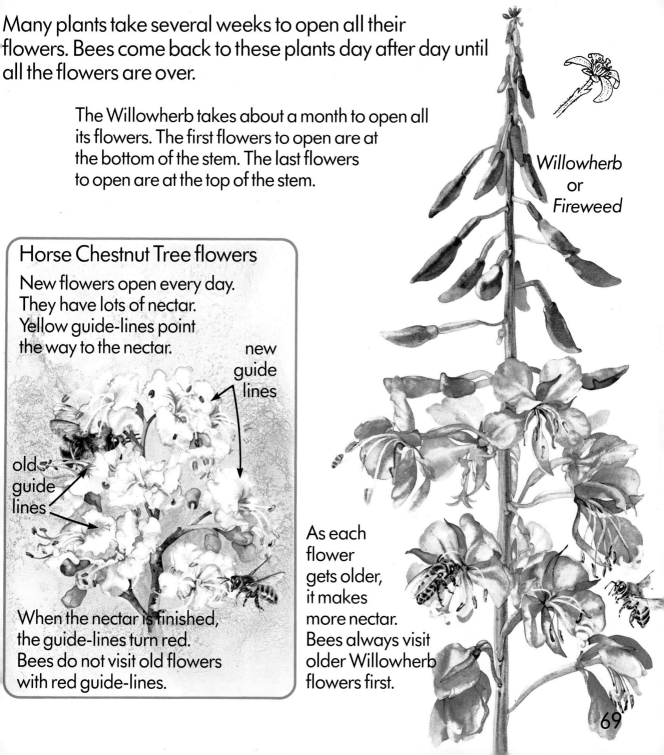

Willowherb or Fireweed

Horse Chestnut Tree flowers

New flowers open every day. They have lots of nectar. Yellow guide-lines point the way to the nectar.

new guide lines

old guide lines

When the nectar is finished, the guide-lines turn red. Bees do not visit old flowers with red guide-lines.

As each flower gets older, it makes more nectar. Bees always visit older Willowherb flowers first.

69

Keeping pollen safe

Most flowers try to keep their pollen safe and dry. Cold weather, rain and dew could damage the pollen or wash it away.

When flowers are closed, the pollen is kept safe.

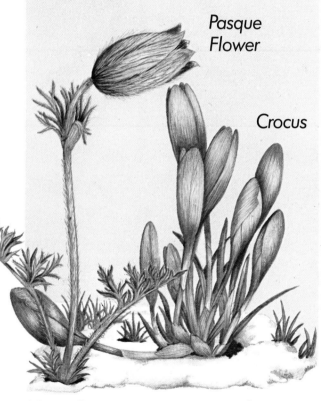

Pasque Flower

Crocus

When flowers are closed, rain and dew cannot get inside.

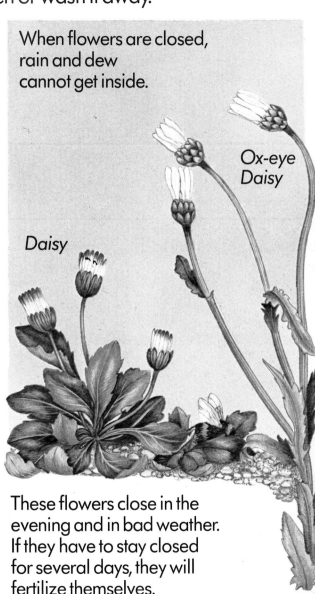

Ox-eye Daisy

Daisy

These flowers come out in early spring. The flowers open only when it is warm and sunny. If the sun goes in, they close up their petals. The flowers open again when the sun comes out.

These flowers close in the evening and in bad weather. If they have to stay closed for several days, they will fertilize themselves.

Harebell

Bugle

Violet

These flowers do not need to close their petals to keep pollen safe. Water cannot collect inside them.

Broom

Petals are closed

Petals open when a bee lands.

The stamens and the pistil of the Broom flower are kept safe inside the petals. They spring out when a bee lands on the bottom petals.

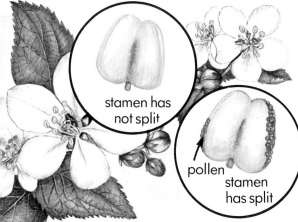

stamen has not split

pollen

stamen has split

Ripe stamens of Apple Tree flowers split open to let out the pollen. The stamens will split open only on warm days.

moth

New Catchfly flowers open in the evening. This is when moths visit them. But if the evenings are very cold, no new flowers will open.

71

Picture puzzle

There are nine flowers and nine fruits on this page. Can you guess which fruits belong to which flowers?

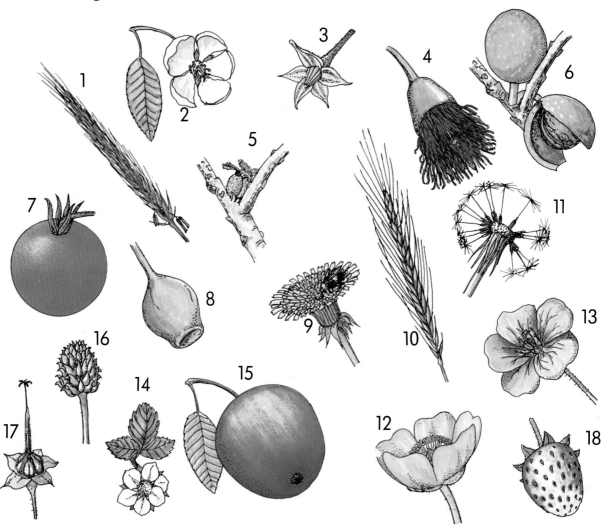

Answers: 1 and 10 Rye. 2 and 15 Apple. 3 and 7 Tomato. 4 and 8 Red Flowering Gum Tree. 5 and 6 Walnut. 9 and 11 Dandelion. 12 and 16 Buttercup. 13 and 17 Cranesbill. 14 and 18 Strawberry.

72

BUTTERFLIES
AND MOTHS

Games

2. Watch the butterfly move

Hold the Butterfly pages like this.

1. Hunt the little green caterpillar

Can you find 11 caterpillars like this in the Butterfly pages?

Watch the top right hand corner and flick the pages over fast.

watch here

Looking at butterflies and moths

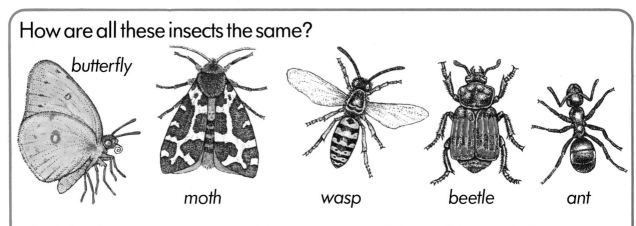

How are all these insects the same?

butterfly

moth　*wasp*　*beetle*　*ant*

Their bodies are made up of three parts and they all have six legs.

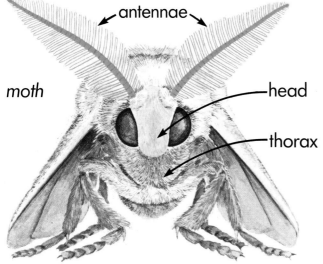

moth

antennae

head

thorax

Butterflies and moths have hooks
on their feet for holding on tight.
They feel and smell with their
long antennae.

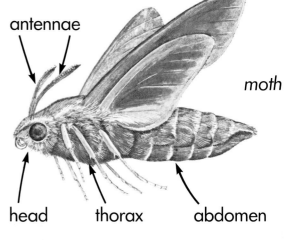

antennae

moth

head　thorax　abdomen

Behind the head is the thorax.
The wings join on to the thorax.
The long part of the body is
called the abdomen.

74

Some insects have four wings, some have two wings and some have no wings. How many wings have butterflies and moths got?

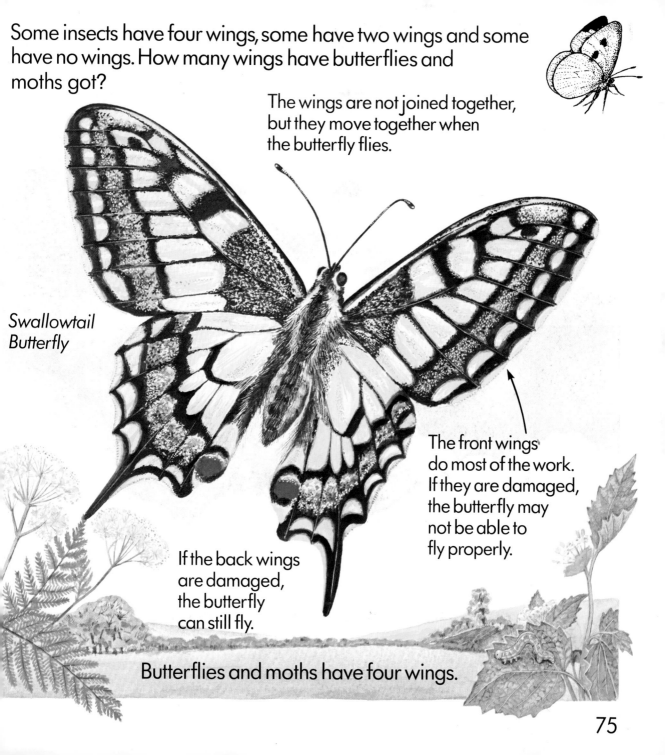

The wings are not joined together, but they move together when the butterfly flies.

Swallowtail Butterfly

The front wings do most of the work. If they are damaged, the butterfly may not be able to fly properly.

If the back wings are damaged, the butterfly can still fly.

Butterflies and moths have four wings.

Looking at wings

Red Underwing Moth

When butterflies rest, they usually close their wings above their backs.

When moths rest, they fold their wings over their backs, or spread them out flat.

Oleander Hawk Moth

Common Blue Butterfly

The wings of a butterfly or moth are often one colour on the outside and a different colour on the inside.

Privet Hawk Moth

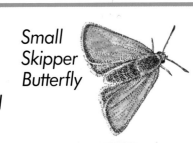

When butterflies and moths rest, the colour of the outside of their wings makes it hard for enemies to see them.

Walnut Moth

Lappet Moth

Scallop Shell Moth

Small Skipper Butterfly

Buff-tip Moth

Some butterflies look like dead leaves when they rest. They are hard to see.

Some moths look like twigs when they rest. It is hard for enemies to see them.

What makes the colours on their wings?

scales

butterfly

moth

Brimstone Butterfly

Red Admiral Butterfly

The wings are covered with coloured or shiny scales. If you touch the wings the scales will rub off.

Grayling Butterfly

Green Hairstreak Butterfly

Monarch Butterfly

77

Keeping warm and feeding

Butterflies and moths need to be warm for their bodies to work properly. When the air is cold, they rest.

Butterflies warm up in the sun.

Titania's Fritillary

The dark parts of the wings warm up quickly. Butterflies from cold countries often have dark colours on their wings.

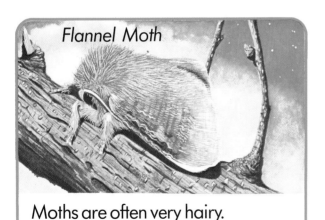

Flannel Moth

Moths are often very hairy. The hairs on their bodies help to keep them warm at night.

Elephant Hawk Moth

Moths often shiver before they fly. The shivering helps to warm up their bodies.

Butterflies and moths do not eat to grow larger.
They use food to make heat inside their bodies.
Heat makes energy. This keeps their bodies working.

*Hummingbird
Hawk Moth*

Moths and butterflies drink
a sweet liquid from flowers.
This liquid is called nectar.

They drink nectar through
a long tube called
a proboscis.

proboscis

*Union Jack
Butterfly*
Some butterflies
can taste
with their feet.

*Lime
Hawk Moth*

sap

Moths may drink sap from
trees or damaged plants.

proboscis

When butterflies and moths
are not feeding, their
proboscis is curled up.

79

A butterfly's day

Common Blue Butterfly

female

1. The butterfly rests at night when it is cold.

2. When the sun comes out, she warms up.

3. She looks for a place to lay her eggs.

4. She lays her eggs on a special plant.

A moth's night

Privet Hawk Moth

male

1. The moth hides in the day.

2. At dusk he shivers to warm himself up.

3. He flies away to find a female.

4. He drinks some nectar from a flower.

5. She warms up again in the sun.

6. Now she is warm enough to fly away.

7. She lands on a flower to drink nectar.

8. When it gets dark and cold, she hides.

5. Now it is very cold so he rests.

6. When it gets warmer, he flies away.

7. He finds a female and mates with her.

8. When it gets light, he hides.

Finding a partner

The most important thing that a butterfly or moth has to do is to find a partner for mating. When a female has mated she will lay her eggs.

male

Scarce Copper Butterflies

female

male

Purple Hairstreak Butterflies

female

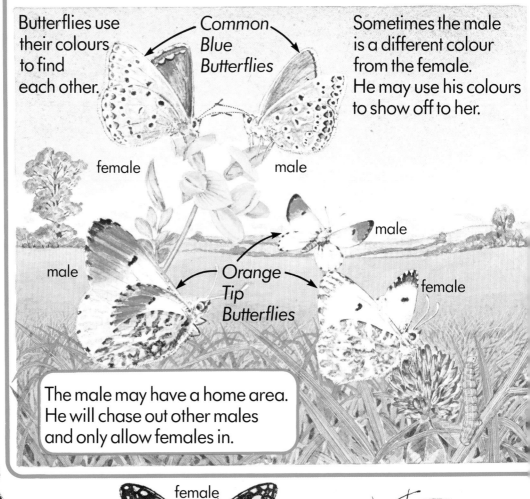

Butterflies use their colours to find each other.

Common Blue Butterflies

Sometimes the male is a different colour from the female. He may use his colours to show off to her.

female

male

male

male

Orange Tip Butterflies

female

The male may have a home area. He will chase out other males and only allow females in.

female

Swallowtail Butterflies

male

You can often tell a male moth from a female moth by his larger antennae.

Emperor Moths

female

male

At night, moths cannot use colour to find each other. Instead the male finds the female by her scent. Each kind of moth has a different scent.

male

Muslin Moths

female

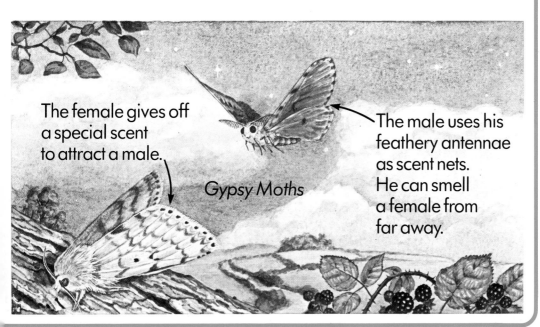

The female gives off a special scent to attract a male.

Gypsy Moths

The male uses his feathery antennae as scent nets. He can smell a female from far away.

male

Hag Moths

female

Oak Eggar Moths

male

female

83

Mating and laying eggs

A pair of butterflies may play together before they mate.
This is called courtship.

The male is holding
the antennae
of the female
between
his wings.

antennae

The female uses
her antennae to
smell a scent
on the wings
of the male.

*Grayling
Butterfly*

When butterflies or moths mate, they join their abdomens together.
A bag of sperm passes from the male to the female.
The sperm joins with eggs inside the female.

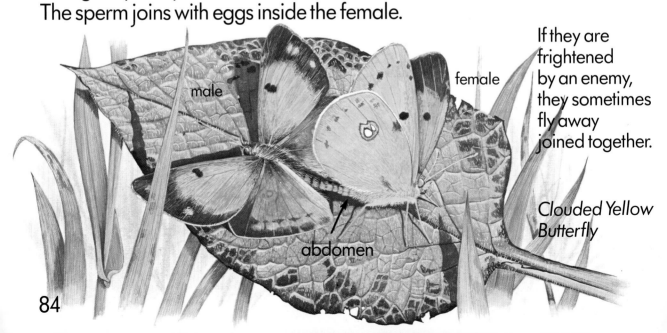

male

female

If they are
frightened
by an enemy,
they sometimes
fly away
joined together.

*Clouded Yellow
Butterfly*

abdomen

A female may have hundreds of eggs inside her. She will lay her eggs when she has mated.

Nettle leaf

eggs

Map Butterfly

A butterfly or moth usually lays her eggs on a special plant. She can lay lots of eggs together, or one egg at a time.

Bulrush Wainscot Moth

abdomen

This moth lays each egg inside a Bulrush. She makes holes in the stem with spines on the end of her abdomen.

Lackey Moth

Leopard Moth

Marbled White Butterfly

egg

This Moth sticks her eggs round a twig.

This Moth sticks her eggs on to tree bark.

This Butterfly lays her eggs as she flies.

The hungry caterpillar

Out of each egg comes a caterpillar. It eats and eats, and grows and grows. When it is big enough to start changing into an adult butterfly or moth, it stops growing.

1. A moth caterpillar is inside this egg.

2. The caterpillar eats a hole in the egg and crawls out.

3. It is very hungry, so it eats the old egg shell.

4. It eats the top of the leaf. Soon the caterpillar grows too big for its skin.

5. The skin splits and the caterpillar wriggles out. It is wearing a new skin.

old skin

Privet Hawk Moth caterpillar

6. The caterpillar eats Privet leaves. It eats and grows and eats and grows. It changes its skin three more times.

The caterpillar cannot see very well. It has twelve tiny eyes on its head. The eyes are too small for you to see.

Mouth parts for chewing.

The three pairs of front legs hold on to the food.

The five pairs of fleshy legs are called claspers. They can grip tightly to a stalk.

The caterpillar breathes through air holes in the side of its body. There is an air hole in the centre of each coloured spot.

87

Caterpillars and pupae

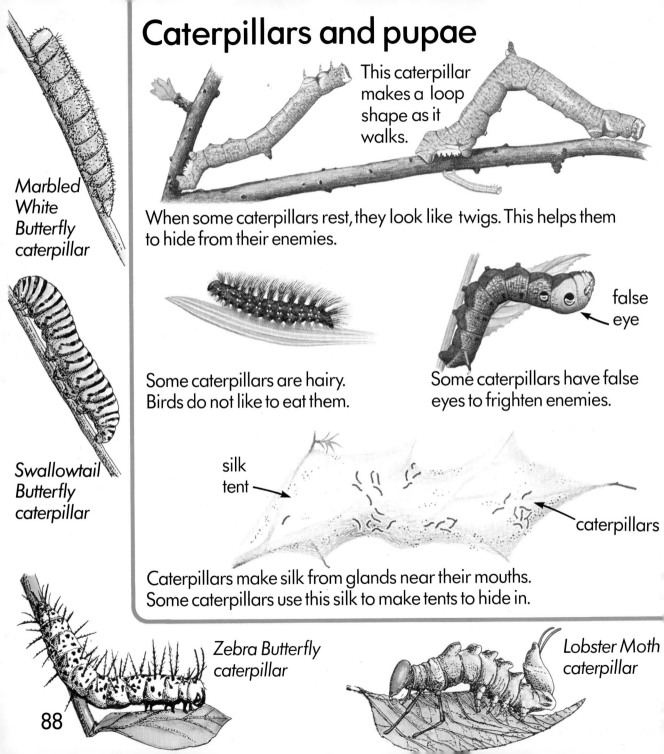

This caterpillar makes a loop shape as it walks.

When some caterpillars rest, they look like twigs. This helps them to hide from their enemies.

Marbled White Butterfly caterpillar

Swallowtail Butterfly caterpillar

Some caterpillars are hairy. Birds do not like to eat them.

false eye

Some caterpillars have false eyes to frighten enemies.

silk tent

caterpillars

Caterpillars make silk from glands near their mouths. Some caterpillars use this silk to make tents to hide in.

Zebra Butterfly caterpillar

Lobster Moth caterpillar

When caterpillars are fully grown, they change into pupae.

Peacock Butterfly caterpillar

old skin

pupa

1. When this caterpillar is fully grown, it hangs upside down.

2. The caterpillar changes into a pupa inside its skin.

3. When the pupa wriggles, the skin splits. and slides up the pupa.

Cabbage White Butterfly pupa

4. The pupa skin is now hard. It has changed colour.

Some moth caterpillars bury themselves in the ground. Then they change into pupae.

silk cocoon

Some moth caterpillars spin silk cocoons around themselves. The caterpillars change into pupae inside the cocoons.

Bagworm Moth cocoon

Convolvulus Hawk Moth pupa

Orange Tip Butterfly pupa

89

The magic change

Inside a pupa, a butterfly or moth is being made.

Monarch Butterfly pupa

The abdomen is being made here.

One wing is being made here.

One antenna is being made here.

One eye is being made here.

1. This pupa is two days old. A Monarch Butterfly is being made inside it.

2. The pupa is now two weeks old. The Butterfly is nearly ready to come out.

The Butterfly is pulling out its antennae, legs and proboscis.

3. The pupa skin splits. The head and legs of the Butterfly come out first.

At first,
the wings
are crumpled.

veins

The proboscis
is in
two parts.

4. The Butterfly pulls out its abdomen. It pumps blood into the veins of its wings.

5. Blood is pumping from the abdomen into the veins. This makes the wings unfold.

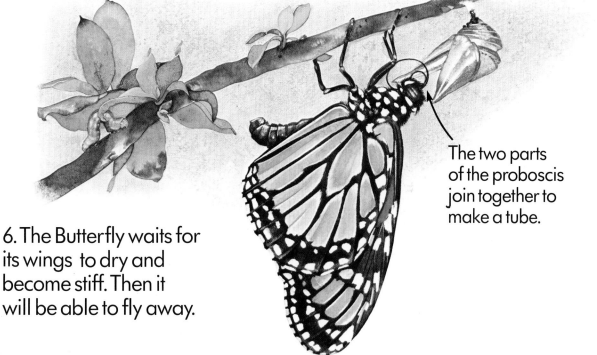

The two parts
of the proboscis
join together to
make a tube.

6. The Butterfly waits for its wings to dry and become stiff. Then it will be able to fly away.

91

How long do they live?

A butterfly or moth goes through four stages in its life. Adult butterflies and moths usually live only a few days or weeks. When they have mated and the female has laid her eggs, the adults die.

1. A butterfly or moth starts its life as an egg.

2. The egg changes into a caterpillar.

3. The caterpillar changes into a pupa.

4. The pupa changes into an adult.

In tropical countries, where the weather is always hot, a butterfly or moth often takes only a few weeks to change from an egg into an adult.

In colder countries, a butterfly or moth may take several months to change from an egg to an adult. In countries with very cold winters, they go into a deep sleep. They wake up when the weather gets warmer.

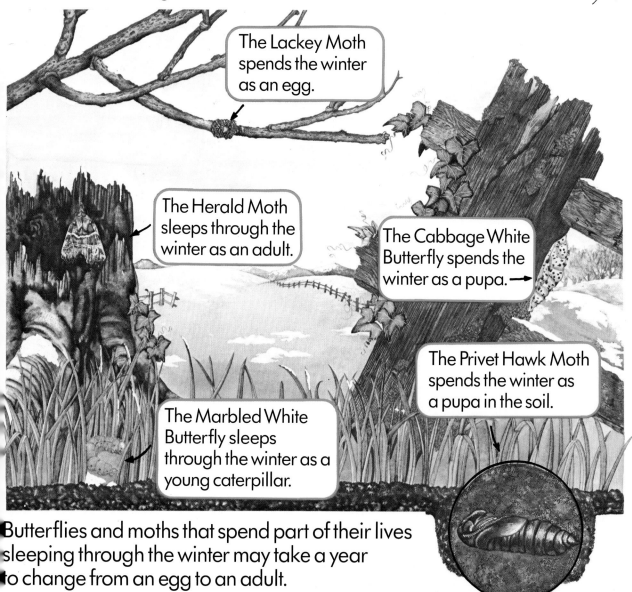

The Lackey Moth spends the winter as an egg.

The Herald Moth sleeps through the winter as an adult.

The Cabbage White Butterfly spends the winter as a pupa. ➡

The Privet Hawk Moth spends the winter as a pupa in the soil.

The Marbled White Butterfly sleeps through the winter as a young caterpillar.

Butterflies and moths that spend part of their lives sleeping through the winter may take a year to change from an egg to an adult.

Enemies

Butterflies and moths have lots of enemies.

Birds eat them.

Spiders eat them.

Insects eat them.

At night, many moths are eaten by bats.

Some moths have ears on the sides of their bodies. They help them to hear the squeaks that bats make. If these moths hear a bat coming, they drop to the ground or try to dodge out of the way.

Blue Underwing Moth

Some butterflies and moths have special colours.
They use them to frighten away enemies.

Red Underwing Moth

Owl Butterfly

If an enemy disturbs this moth, it opens and closes its wings. The flash of red may frighten away the enemy.

This butterfly has false eyes on its wings. Birds may think they are the eyes of a dangerous animal.

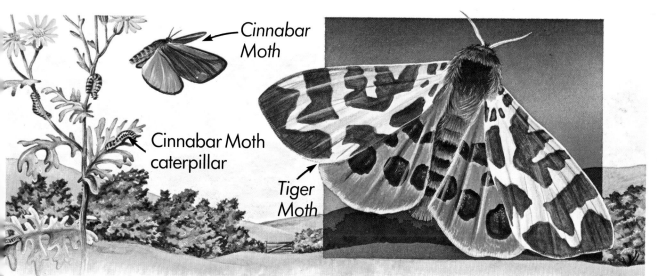

Cinnabar Moth

Cinnabar Moth caterpillar

Tiger Moth

Most butterflies and moths that are red and black, or yellow and black, taste nasty. Birds learn to leave them alone.

At night, Tiger Moths make clicking noises. Bats soon learn that moths that make this noise taste bad.

95

Picture puzzle

There are four butterflies, three moths and four caterpillars hidden in this picture. How many can you find?

WILD
ANIMALS

A Wood Mouse is hidden near this Leopard. Can you find 15 more Wood Mice hidden in this section of the book?

Looking at mammals

Mammals are different from all the other animals in the world. They are the only animals that have fur or hair. Female mammals are the only animals that produce milk to feed to their young. You are a mammal.

Fallow Deer feeding her fawn.

All mammals breathe air, even mammals that live in water.

A mammal has a good brain.

A mammal makes the inside of its body stay at about the same temperature — even when it is hot or cold outside.

All mammals have some fur or hair on their body.

▲ Musk Oxen have lots of hair. This keeps them warm.

Porcupines have special hairs, called quills.

Elephants ► have only a few hairs.

Many mammals have two kinds of hair in their coat. Beavers have a thick layer of short, soft hairs under a layer of long, rough hairs. Only the long hairs get wet in water.

Bactrian Camel

Some mammals, such as Camels, grow two new coats every year. This Camel is growing its thin summer coat. Its thick winter coat falls out so fast that the hairs come off in large chunks.

winter coat

summer coat

Legs and feet

Most mammals move around on four legs.

ankle

Pandas walk on their whole foot.

ankle

Foxes walk on their toes.

ankle

Deer walk on their toe nails.

Back feet land in front of front feet.

Otters use their tail to change direction.

Mountain Hares have feet like snowshoes. Their feet are wide and flat and have lots of fur underneath. This helps them to walk or run over the snow without sinking in very far.

Otters have skin between their toes. They use their feet like flippers to push them through the water.

100

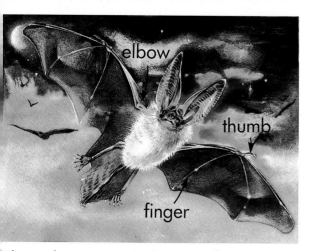

The only mammals that can fly are bats. They use their arms as wings. Each wing is made of skin. The skin is stretched over the bones of the arms and fingers.

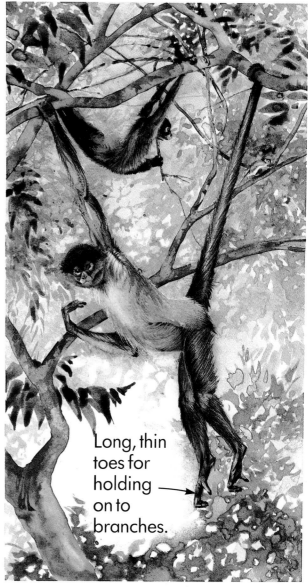

Long, thin toes for holding on to branches.

Kangaroo Rats hop around on two legs. They use their long back legs to make huge leaps. Their tail helps them to balance.

Spider Monkeys use their strong tail like an extra arm or leg. They curl the tip of the tail around branches to help them swing through the trees.

Teeth and feeding

Many mammals feed mainly on plants. They have a lot of grinding teeth because plants are hard to chew.

Chipmunks carry food in cheek pouches.

Horny pad is under here.

The front teeth of a Chipmunk never stop growing. Its teeth do not get too long as it wears them down when it feeds.

Bighorn Sheep have no front teeth in their top jaw. Instead they have a horny pad to bite off the tops of plants

Long tongue pulls leaves off branches.

Zebra

Dik-dik

Eland

Giraffe

Many different mammals can feed close together on the African grasslands. This is because they eat different kinds of plants and feed at different heights. You can see this if you look carefully at the mammals in the picture above.

fruit

Dead
Vole

Long, sensitive
fingers help
to find and
catch food.

fish

Koalas feed only on the leaves of Gum Trees. They will die if they cannot find the right sort of Gum Tree to feed on.

Racoons feed on plants and animals. They eat living things and dead things. They can usually find enough to eat.

Long, pointed teeth to grip an animal's throat and strangle it.

Cheetah

Gazelle

Razor-sharp cheek teeth to tear meat.

Some mammals feed mainly on other animals. They use up a lot of energy catching their food. Cheetahs may be too tired to eat for up to 15 minutes after they have killed an animal. But meat is very nourishing, so they do not feed every day.

Mammals at night

More than half the mammals in the world come out at night.

Potto

Pupil opens wide to let in lots of light.

Sticky pads on toes help to grip branches.

Many mammals have a special layer at the back of their eyes. This layer helps them to see in the dark. It makes their eyes glow if a light shines on them.

The Tarsier has huge eyes and special ears that help it to see and hear well at night. It leaps through the trees and pounces on insects and small animals.

Badgers use their sharp sense of smell and good hearing to move around and feed at night. They find food by sniffing the ground with their sensitive noses.

fold of skin

Many bats feed on the insects that come out at night. This Greater Horseshoe Bat eats flies, beetles and moths. It has sharp pointed teeth to chop up its food.

Sugar Gliders feed on flowers and insects at night. They stretch open the folds of skin along the sides of their bodies to glide quietly from tree to tree.

The Red Fox hunts at night. When it hears and smells a mouse in the grass, the Fox leaps up in the air like this. It will land with its front paws on the mouse.

Escaping from enemies

sharp scales →

Squirrels escape from enemies by climbing trees. They are small and light and can leap on to very thin branches. Most of their enemies cannot follow.

Pangolins have horny scales like a suit of armour. The back edge of each scale is sharp. When they roll into a tight ball, their enemies cannot hurt them.

1. This Spiny Anteater has sharp spines on its back. It burrows into the ground to escape enemies.

2. It digs straight down with its long claws and sinks out of sight in about one minute.

3. When it is buried, its enemies leave it alone. The spines may cut them if they try to dig it up.

Skunk holds tail up to say "Go away or I will squirt you with smelly liquid".

summer

winter

Skunks squirt a nasty liquid at enemies. The liquid comes from a gland under the tail. Most enemies leave them alone.

The Mountain Hare lives in places where it snows in winter. It has a white coat in winter and a brown coat in summer. This helps it to hide from enemies, such as Foxes.

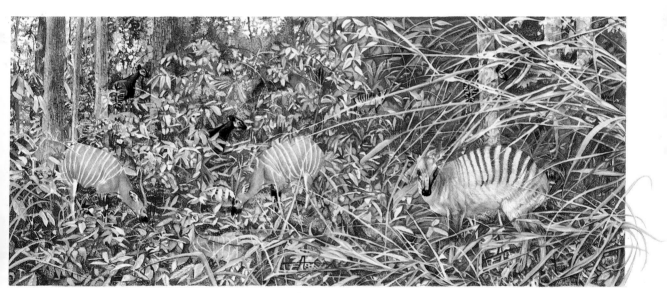

Many mammals that live in forests or jungles have stripes or spots on their fur. They match the colours and patterns on the trees and bushes. This helps them to hide from their enemies. There are eight mammals in this African jungle. Can you find them all?

Homes

Mammals build homes to keep them warm, dry and safe from enemies

Rabbits live in a maze of tunnels, which they dig under the ground. Their home is called a warren. They run into the warren to escape from enemies.

The female Harvest Mouse builds a home for her young. She tears grass leaves into strips and weaves them into a round nest. It is warm and dry inside.

The cubs are born in the middle of winter.

The female Polar Bear digs a cave of ice and snow to spend the winter in. She does not come out until the weather gets warmer in spring.

molehill

The only home Chimpanzees make is a nest to sleep in. They build the nest near the top of a tree. They bend branches over to make a cushion of leaves.

A Mole spends most of its life inside its home. It uses its front feet like shovels to dig out tunnels in the soil. It feeds and sleeps in these tunnels.

air hole

The home is called a lodge.

This is what a Beaver's home looks like inside. The young are safe from enemies.

underwater entrances

Finding a mate

female

male

Siberian Tiger

male

female

Female mammals often give off a special smell when they are ready to mate. A male Harvest Mouse sniffs a female to see if she is ready to mate.

Tigers play together before they mate. This female is asking the male to mate with her. She bites him gently and then rubs her body against his.

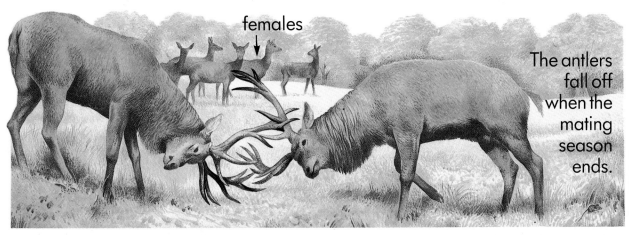

females

The antlers fall off when the mating season ends.

Once a year, a male Red Deer rounds up a group of females for mating. He roars loudly to tell other males how strong he is. If another male roars as often as he does, they fight with their antlers. The strongest male wins the females.

Male antelopes, such as this Uganda Kob, have to dance in front of a female before they mate with her.

male   female   male   female

1. The male Kob holds his head up to show off the white patch under his chin. He stretches out his front legs to show off his black stripes.

2. Then he holds his front leg out very stiff and straight. He taps the female's side gently. If she stands still, he will mate with her.

Male and female Red Foxes dance together before they mate. They stand on their back legs and hug each other with their front legs. They hold their mouths open and make a chattering call.

Eggs and birth

After a female mammal has mated, a baby may start to grow inside her. Most baby mammals stay inside their mother until they have grown all the parts of their bodies. Then they are ready to be born.

When Zebras are born, they can see, hear and smell and have hair all over their bodies. They can run about an hour after they are born. They stay close to the other Zebras. This helps to keep them safe from enemies.

birth sac

When Dormice are born, they are helpless. They are blind and deaf and have no hair on their bodies. They are born in a nest, which helps to keep them warm and safe from enemies.

A few mammals are born before they grow all the parts of their bodies. Most of them finish developing in a pouch on their mother's body.

pouch

Close-up of the birth opening. The baby climbs upwards.

As soon as a baby Kangaroo is born, it has to crawl from the birth opening up to its mother's pouch. This takes about three minutes. The baby is so small, it would fit into a teaspoon.

Looking inside the pouch

The baby holds on to a teat and sucks milk from its mother. It stays in the pouch for six months. By then, it has grown all the parts of its body.

The Platypus and the Spiny Anteaters are unusual mammals that lay eggs. A baby grows inside each egg.

The Platypus lays her eggs in a nest of leaves and grass. The eggs have a soft shell.

The nest is at the end of a long burrow in a river bank.

Growing up

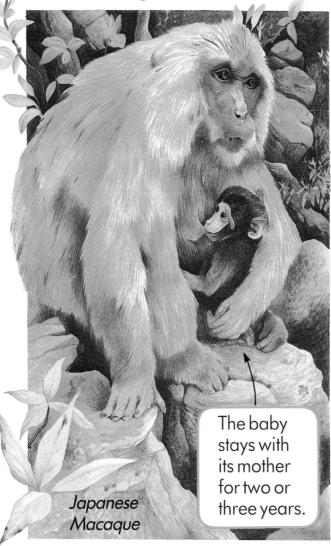

Japanese
Macaque

The baby stays with its mother for two or three years.

White-tailed
Deer

Most mammals spend a lot of time licking their young. This keeps them clean and healthy. It also forms a bond between mother and young.

A baby mammal sucks milk from glands on its mother's body. The glands produce milk as soon as a baby is born. The milk is rich in foods the baby needs.

A Tigress picks up her cubs in her mouth to carry them to a safe place. The cubs do not get hurt as they keep still and their mother's jaws do not shut properly

114

African Elephant

Mountain Goats play games with their mother and the other young goats. This helps them to learn how to balance and climb on the steep mountain slopes.

This mother Elephant is protecting her calf from an enemy. The young Elephant is too small to look after itself. It stays close to its mother.

White-toothed Shrews go out with their mother when they are about a week old. They hold on to each other in a long line so they do not get lost.

Living in a group

Lions live in a group called a pride. The female Lions are called Lionesses. They do most of the hunting. They also feed the cubs and look after them. The male Lions keep a safe area for the pride to live in.

An adult male has a thick mane. This protects his head and neck in fights. It also helps him to attract a female.

Lionesses hunt in teams. They are more likely to catch large animals if they hunt together.

This is a young male. He will leave the pride when he is about three years old.

The cubs spend a lot of time playing. This helps them learn how to fight and hunt.

A Lioness usually stays in the pride for life. She may feed any of the cubs. This helps them survive.

Chimpanzees live in a group called a community. The males defend the group from enemies. They often travel and feed with other males. Females look after the young.

A Chimpanzee may share its food with other Chimps in the group. One Chimp may stare at another to ask for food.

There is a top male in each group. He often charges about like this making a lot of noise. This shows the other Chimps he is in charge.

Chimps crouch down like this when they meet a more important Chimp. This Chimp may pat them to say "I will not attack you".

Woodland Chimps catch Termites by poking a grass stem into their nest. Young Chimps watch their parents to find out how to do this.

Chimpanzees spend a lot of time grooming their fur. This helps to keep them clean and healthy. Grooming also calms the Chimps and helps them to stay good friends.

Sea Mammals

The only mammals that spend their whole lives in the sea are Dolphins, Whales and Sea Cows. They have few hairs and no back legs.

A Dolphin comes to the surface to breathe air through its blowhole.

A Dolphin's teeth are all the same. They are good for catching fish.

A Dolphin's body is a good shape for moving fast through the water. It moves its strong tail up and down to push it along. It uses its flippers and the fin on its back to change direction.

Mouth of a Humpback Whale.

bony plates

Manatees are a kind of Sea Cow.

Some Whales have no teeth. Instead they have rows of bony plates, which end in a thick, hairy fringe. The fringe strains tiny animals from the sea water.

This Manatee calf is sucking milk from a teat near its mother's flipper. Manatees are born in the water and can swim as soon as they are born.

Seals, Sea Lions and Walruses spend only part of their lives in the sea. They have back legs and most of them have a coat of short hair.

Long toes with skin between them.

tail

A Sea Lion's smooth, thin body helps it to swim fast underwater. It uses its front flippers to push it along. It uses its back flippers to change direction. It has only a short tail.

Walruses use their long teeth to dig up shellfish from the sea floor. They also use their teeth for fighting.

Pups grow fast on their mother's rich milk.

A layer of skin comes off with the old fur coat.

Seals, Sea Lions and Walruses come out of the sea every year to give birth, mate and grow a new coat of fur.
This is a group of Elephant Seals. The males fight each other to win their own area on the beach. They will mate with all the females in their area.

119

Picture puzzle

The Rabbit has to get back to his home on the other side of the maze. Can you help him to find the right path? Part of the maze goes through the Giraffe's body. Can you name all the mammals in the maze?

START →

HOME

120

FISHES

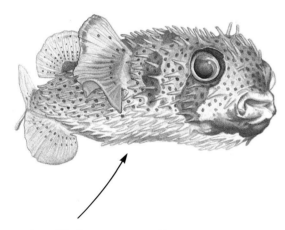

Porcupine Fishes normally
look like this.

When they are frightened, they
can blow themselves up with
water like this. Then other
fishes are less likely to eat them.

What is a fish?

Fishes are animals that live in water. They breathe through gills and have a skeleton inside the body. Their bodies usually stay at the same temperature as the water around them. Most fishes lay eggs.

The gills are under the gill cover.

Goldfish eggs

Goldfish

The skeleton supports the body and fins.

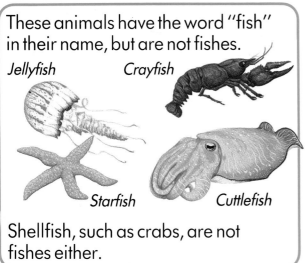

These animals have the word "fish" in their name, but are not fishes.

Jellyfish

Crayfish

Starfish

Cuttlefish

Shellfish, such as crabs, are not fishes either.

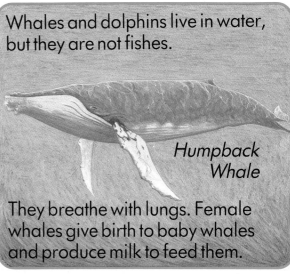

Whales and dolphins live in water, but they are not fishes.

Humpback Whale

They breathe with lungs. Female whales give birth to baby whales and produce milk to feed them.

There are three main kinds of fishes.

1. Bony fishes

Most fishes have a
skeleton made of bone.
Their bodies are usually
covered by very thin scales.

Bony fishes
have a
gill
cover.

Thin, overlapping
scales.

Perch

2. Sharks and Rays

scales

Skate (a type of ray)

These openings
lead to the
gills.

Blue
Shark

Gill
openings

scales

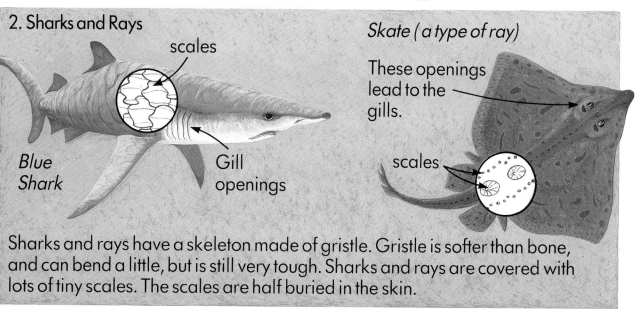

Sharks and rays have a skeleton made of gristle. Gristle is softer than bone,
and can bend a little, but is still very tough. Sharks and rays are covered with
lots of tiny scales. The scales are half buried in the skin.

3. Lampreys

Gill openings

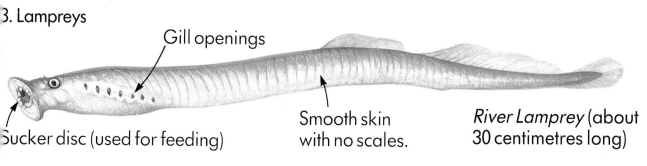

Smooth skin
with no scales.

River Lamprey (about
30 centimetres long)

Sucker disc (used for feeding)

Lampreys have no jaws and no scales. The skeleton is made of gristle.

How fishes move

Most fishes swim using their fins. Some fins move the body forward. Others help to keep the fish the right way up.

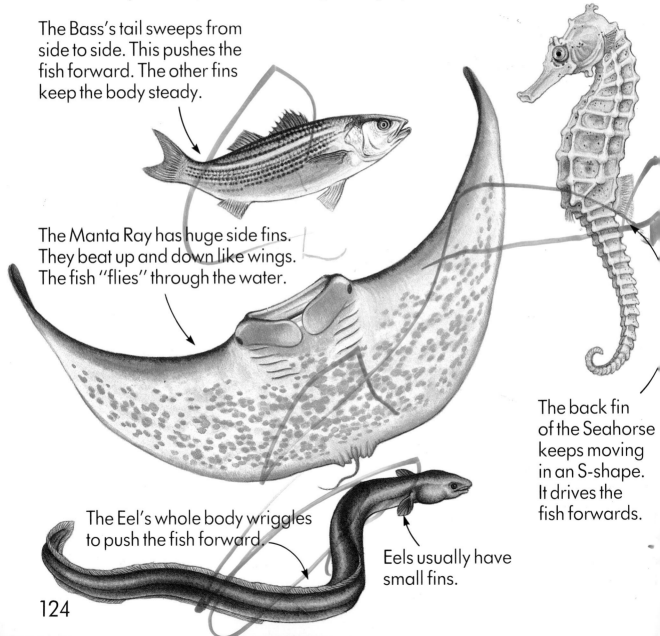

The Bass's tail sweeps from side to side. This pushes the fish forward. The other fins keep the body steady.

The Manta Ray has huge side fins. They beat up and down like wings. The fish "flies" through the water.

The back fin of the Seahorse keeps moving in an S-shape. It drives the fish forwards.

The Eel's whole body wriggles to push the fish forward.

Eels usually have small fins.

Some fishes move in unusual ways.

South American freshwater Hatchet Fish

Long side fin

Flying Fishes are chased by dolphins and sharks.

Long side fins

Some Hatchet Fishes can leap from the water. They fly through the air by beating their fins very fast. As they do this, the fins make a buzzing sound.

Flying Fishes swim very fast under the water using the tail fin. Suddenly they burst through the surface and spread out their fins. They glide in the air.

long fins

Mud-skippers leave the water to catch insects on land.

They carry water in their gills for breathing.

Frogfishes have fins at the ends of four short "arms". They crawl about amongst coral and seaweed looking for food.

Mud-skippers can jump. They curl the tail around against the mud. Suddenly they jerk the body straight. The whole fish jumps forwards.

How fishes breathe

Fishes need a gas called oxygen to live. There is oxygen in the water, and most fishes get it by using their gills. The blood inside the gills takes up oxygen from the water.

gill cover

Trout

The gills look like this when the gill cover is taken away. They are bright red because they contain a lot of blood.

The pictures below show how most fishes breathe.

Mouth open
WATER

1. The fish gulps a big mouthful of water. Then it closes its mouth.

Mouth shut

2. This pushes the water between the gills. The blood in the gills takes up the oxygen.

Mouth shut

3. The blood carries oxygen around the body. The water comes out through the gill opening.

126

mouth

gill slits

Underside of
Thornback Ray.

Water enters
through holes.

eyes

Thornback Ray
resting
on the sand.

The mouth of a ray is on the underside of its body. When the ray rests on the sand, it cannot gulp a mouthful of clean water. Instead, it takes in water through two holes on top of its head. The water goes down over the gills and is pumped out through the gill slits.

Lungfishes have lungs as well as gills.

African Lungfishes usually live underwater in lakes. They use their gills and lungs to breathe. They gulp air at the surface of the water.

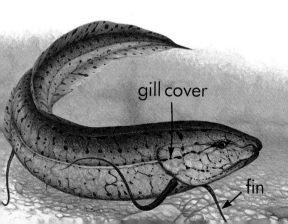

gill cover

fin

In hot weather, the lakes dry up. The Lungfish buries itself in the mud. It uses its lungs to breathe air through a hole.

The fish covers itself in slime.

hole for air

African Lungfish

127

How fishes find their way around

Like us, fishes can smell, see, taste, and hear. They also have special senses to help them find their way around.

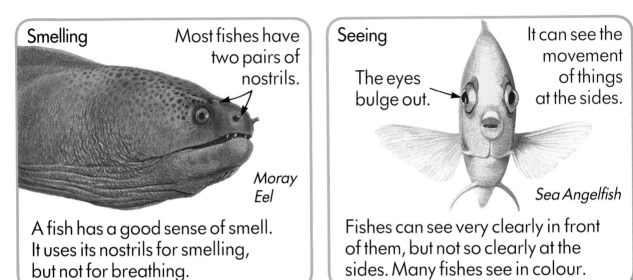

Smelling

Most fishes have two pairs of nostrils.

Moray Eel

A fish has a good sense of smell. It uses its nostrils for smelling, but not for breathing.

Seeing

The eyes bulge out.

It can see the movement of things at the sides.

Sea Angelfish

Fishes can see very clearly in front of them, but not so clearly at the sides. Many fishes see in colour.

Tasting and feeling

Catfish

Some fishes have feelers on their chin and lips. The feelers are called barbels. The fish can taste with its barbels. It can also use them to search for food.

barbel

Hearing

Striped Drum Fish

Lateral line

Carp

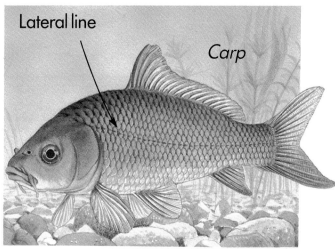

Fishes have ears inside their heads. This fish lives in murky water, so hearing is more important to it than seeing. It finds other Drum Fish by making loud drumming noises.

Most fishes have a line running along each side of their body. It is called the lateral line. The little holes in the line can sense the movements made by other animals in the water.

A few fishes have a special part of the body which makes electricity.

This Elephant Fish can electrify the water around it.

These lines show where the fish sends electricity.

As Elephant Fishes move around, they notice anything which alters this electricity. This stops them from bumping into things. It also helps them to find each other. They can easily swim backwards using this sense.

Ways of catching food

Fishes do not have regular meals. They eat what they can when they can. Some may go without food for days. Others catch food all the time. The shape of a fish's mouth often shows how it catches its food.

Black Swallower

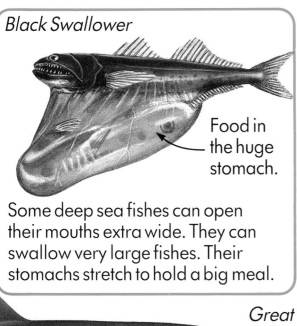

Food in the huge stomach.

Some deep sea fishes can open their mouths extra wide. They can swallow very large fishes. Their stomachs stretch to hold a big meal.

Basking Shark

gill rakers

This shark swims with its mouth wide open. Its throat is lined with curved pieces of gristle called gill rakers. These catch tiny animals.

Great White Shark

The Great White Shark is big and strong. It can catch almost anything in the sea. Its teeth are sharp and triangular. As each tooth wears away or falls out, a new tooth from the row behind it takes its place.

Some fishes catch their food in cunning ways.

*African freshwater
Butterfly Fish*

*Malaysian
Archer Fish*

When the insect falls into the water, the fish eats it.

This fish lies in wait just under the surface of the water. When an insect lands, the fish leaps to grab it.

This fish can spit water at insects and spiders above the surface. The tiny jet of water knocks them off plants.

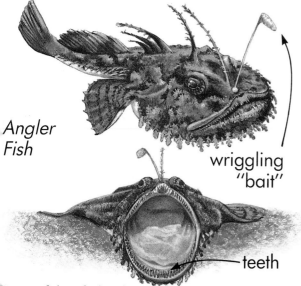

*Angler
Fish*

wriggling "bait"

teeth

Part of this fish's body forms a kind of "fishing rod" and "bait". Small fishes mistake the "bait" for food and come too close. They get caught and eaten.

*American
Garpike*

hundreds of sharp teeth

The Garpike lies quietly at the surface or in the weeds. When a fish comes near, it turns slowly to face its prey, then charges.

131

Colours in fishes

Many fishes are covered with brightly coloured patterns. In their natural surroundings, these markings help them to hide.

The Mackerel's colouring helps it to avoid its enemies, such as birds and big fishes. It is well camouflaged.

It has a dark blue pattern on its back.

Its belly and sides are white.

Mackerel

If you look down on a Mackerel from a boat, its blue back seems to merge with the water.

If you look up at a Mackerel from below, its white belly seems to merge with the sky.

Fishes like this Pike feed on other fishes. It lies in wait amongst the reeds. The blotches on its body blend with the reed stems, making it hard to see.

Many fishes living on the sea bed can change colour as they move about. The colour of this Australian Wobbegong (a shark) matches the sand and gravel.

Some fishes use bright colours or bold markings to trick their enemies or to warn them to keep away.

mouth

Trigger Fish

The mouth seems to be this big.

dark spot

tail

Long-nosed Butterfly Fish

eye

mouth

This Trigger Fish has dark markings on the lips and face. The mouth looks much bigger and fiercer than it really is. Other fishes keep away.

Many Butterfly Fishes have a dark spot near the tail. It looks like an eye. This confuses other fishes because the head seems to be where the tail is.

This fish has spines on its back and is brightly coloured. The spines have poison in them and the colours warn other fishes to keep away.

Lion Fish

133

Finding a mate and making a nest

Most fishes just come together in groups to lay their eggs. In some fishes, however, one male and one female form a pair. The male shows off to the female. This is called displaying.

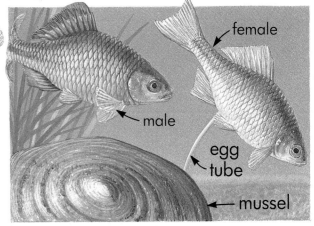

The male Stickleback displays his red belly to the female. This coaxes her to lay her eggs in the nest he has built. He drives other males away.

The male Bitterling displays to the female and leads her to a live mussel. She lays her eggs inside it through a special egg-laying tube.

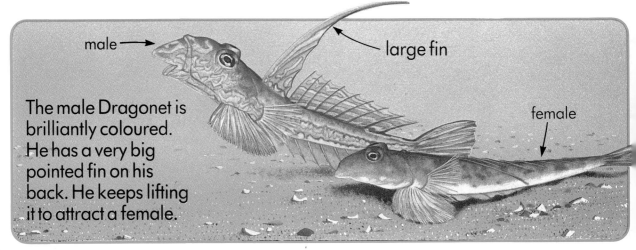

The male Dragonet is brilliantly coloured. He has a very big pointed fin on his back. He keeps lifting it to attract a female.

Some fishes make a nest. Others just hide their eggs. But in both cases, the eggs are safe from being eaten or being washed away by the water.

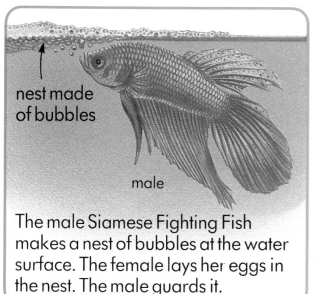

nest made of bubbles

male

The male Siamese Fighting Fish makes a nest of bubbles at the water surface. The female lays her eggs in the nest. The male guards it.

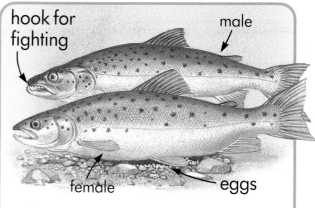

hook for fighting

male

female

eggs

The female Salmon scrapes a nest in the river gravel. The nest is called a redd. Males fight each other to win a female and her redd.

Californian Grunion

These fishes are brought on to the shore by the high tide. They bury their eggs in the sand on the beach.

African Lyretail

male

female

eggs

Lyretails live in small pools which often dry up. They bury their eggs in the mud. The baby fishes do not hatch until it rains again.

Fish eggs and babies

Most fishes lay lots of very small eggs. Some eggs float in the sea, and others stick to plants and rocks. The parents do not usually look after them.

eye

Trout egg

1. Fish eggs have a lot of yolk inside them. The baby grows by feeding on the yolk.

Fins beginning to grow.

yolk

newly-hatched Trout

2. The baby fish has hatched, but it still lives on the stored food in the yolk.

young Trout

3. The yolk lasts until the fins of the young fish are fully grown.

Remains of yolk.

Some fishes lay a few large eggs. Dogfish eggs are laid inside a case which becomes hard in the sea. The case protects the egg as it grows.

Egg case of Dogfish

Dogfish

Some bony fishes look after their eggs until the young hatch out.

female

male

babies

pouch

Male Seahorses carry the female's eggs in a pouch until they hatch.

Baby Guppy being born.

male

The female Guppy keeps her eggs inside her body. The young hatch just before they are born.

eggs

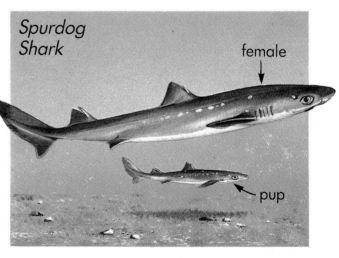

Spurdog Shark

female

pup

Male Tilapias carry the eggs in their mouth. They also shelter the young fishes in their mouth.

Some sharks give birth to babies, called pups. Others lay eggs in a hard egg case and leave them to hatch out.

137

Life in fresh water

Many different kinds of fishes can live in the same river, because they like different parts of the river.

The Trout likes a fast-flowing mountain stream. The water is clean and cold. There is plenty of oxygen in the water.

The Minnow prefers streams which flow more slowly. The water has to be clean.

The Chub likes gently flowing rivers which are deep.

The Bream prefers rivers which flow very slowly.

The water in some streams and rivers flows very fast. The fishes must make sure that they are not swept away by the strong current.

Asian hillstream Loach

water current

Some fishes, like this baby Salmon, hide behind stones to escape the current.

This fish is flat underneath. It can cling to big stones on the bed of the stream.

These fishes are well suited to the places where they live.

South American freshwater Angelfish

Blind Tetra

This Angelfish is very thin. It can swim between plant stems, and hide in them from its enemies.

This fish lives in freshwater lakes in caves. It has no eyes, but it can find its way around in the dark.

Life in the shallow seas

The shallow seas around the seashore have lots of food and hiding places for fishes. Many different kinds of fishes live there.

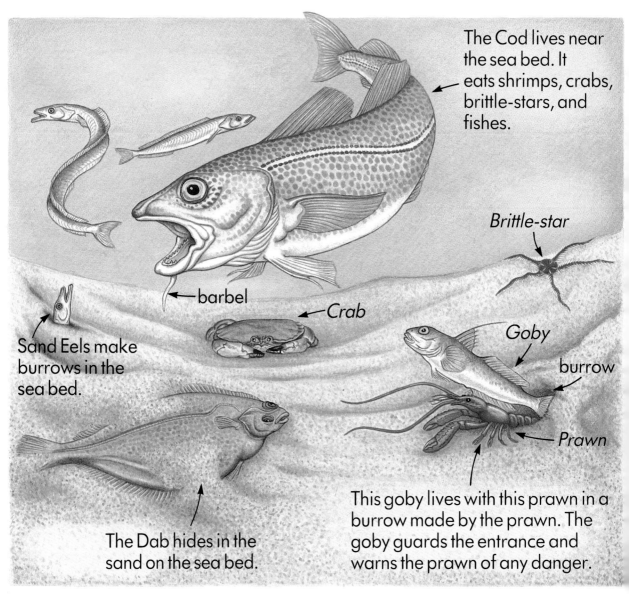

The Cod lives near the sea bed. It eats shrimps, crabs, brittle-stars, and fishes.

Brittle-star

barbel

Crab

Goby

burrow

Sand Eels make burrows in the sea bed.

Prawn

The Dab hides in the sand on the sea bed.

This goby lives with this prawn in a burrow made by the prawn. The goby guards the entrance and warns the prawn of any danger.

A coral reef is the best place to find fishes. They can live or hide all over the reef. Some fishes eat coral, as well as sheltering in it.

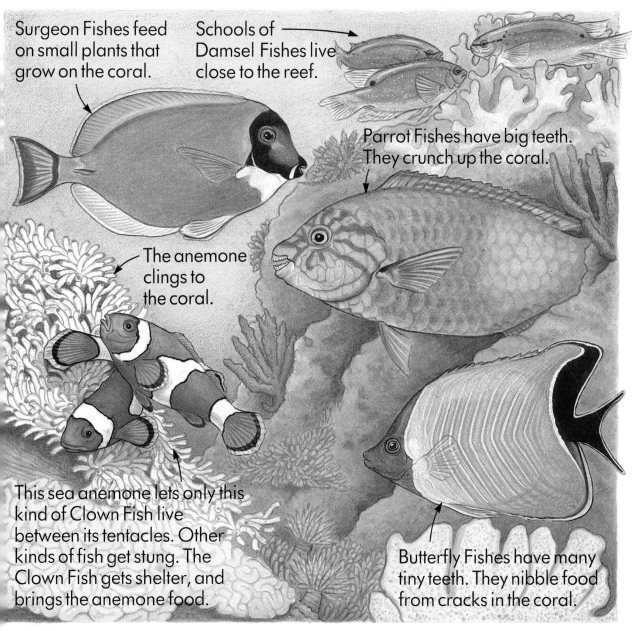

Surgeon Fishes feed on small plants that grow on the coral.

Schools of Damsel Fishes live close to the reef.

Parrot Fishes have big teeth. They crunch up the coral.

The anemone clings to the coral.

This sea anemone lets only this kind of Clown Fish live between its tentacles. Other kinds of fish get stung. The Clown Fish gets shelter, and brings the anemone food.

Butterfly Fishes have many tiny teeth. They nibble food from cracks in the coral.

Life in the deep seas

The deep sea is a bleak place to live. It is dark and very cold. No plants and not many animals live there. The fishes have to make sure they catch whatever food is around.

Viper Fish

teeth

mouth

Gulper Eel

Some fishes, like this Viper Fish, catch their prey with their big teeth.

Others have a mouth that is very big for the size of their body.

Many fishes eat small animals which live on the ocean floor.

Tripod Fish

long fins

Spiny-eel

Rat-tail

The Tripod Fish props itself up on its long fins. The long rays in these fins can sense food buried in the mud.

These two fishes swim with their heads down to find brittle-stars and small shrimps that hide in the sea bed.

Most deep sea fishes are black in colour. Some of them have special parts of their bodies that make light. When these lights are turned off, the fishes disappear into the darkness of the deep sea.

This fish has large eyes, so it can see quite well in the dark. It has no lights. It feeds on tiny shrimp-like animals.

Schools of Lantern Fishes keep together by flashing their lights on and off.

The Dragon Fish has a red light and a green light near each eye. It uses the lights like a torch to find food.

This deep sea Angler Fish has lights on its "fishing rods". It grabs other fishes that are attracted to the lights.

143

Picture puzzle

Each of the fishes drawn here has a tail from one of the other fishes. Can you work out which tail belongs to which body? Do you know the names of the fishes? The answers are at the bottom of the page.

Answers: 1 Mackerel (f). 2 Shark (i). 3 Seahorse (i). 4 Clownfish (a). 5 Eel (e). 6 African freshwater Butterfly Fish (c). 7 Tripod Fish (d). 8 Lamprey (b). 9 Lyretail (j). 10 Gulper Eel (g).

CREEPY CRAWLIES

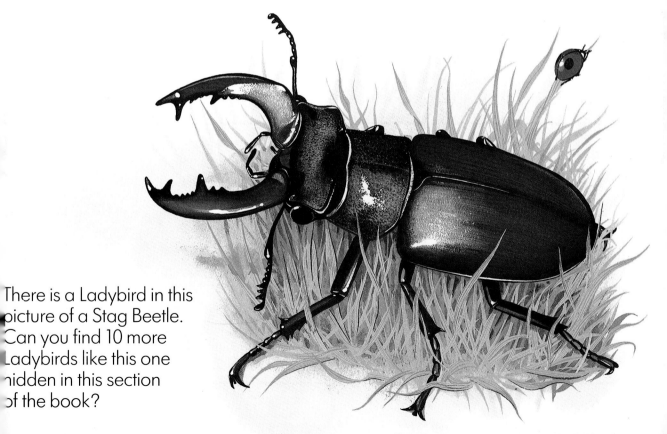

There is a Ladybird in this picture of a Stag Beetle. Can you find 10 more Ladybirds like this one hidden in this section of the book?

Looking at insects and other small animals

This book is about animals called invertebrates, which means "no backbone". They have no skeleton inside their body. Most of the different kinds of invertebrates are insects, but not all. On these pages you can see the six groups of land invertebrates described in this book.

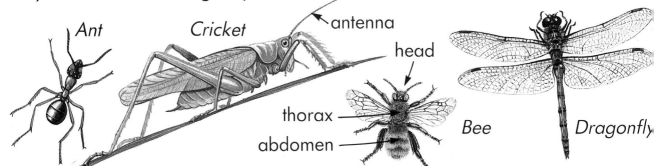

These are just four of the thousands of different kinds of insects. All adult insects have six legs and three parts to their body. They have a head, a middle section called the thorax, and an end section called the abdomen. On the head are two feelers called antennae. Most insects have wings at some stage in their lives.

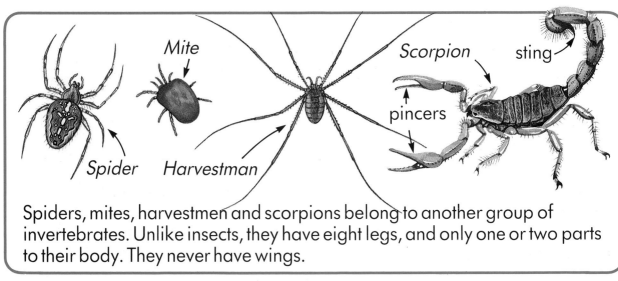

Spiders, mites, harvestmen and scorpions belong to another group of invertebrates. Unlike insects, they have eight legs, and only one or two parts to their body. They never have wings.

Millipedes and centipedes have the most legs of any invertebrate.

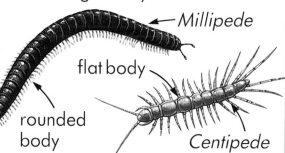

Millipede

flat body

rounded body

Centipede

Their body is divided into a head and many rings, called segments. Most centipedes have 30 legs, while some millipedes have up to 700. They both have feelers.

Woodlice usually have a flat body divided into several segments.

Woodlouse

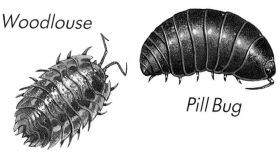

Pill Bug

They have 14 legs that are used for walking and 2 that are used for feeding. Woodlice are also called sow-bugs and slaters. Pill Bugs are woodlice that can roll into a ball.

Worms, like millipedes and centipedes, have many segments in their body.

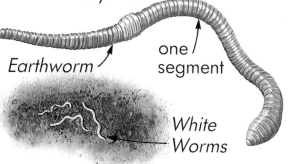

one segment

Earthworm

White Worms

But they have no obvious head, no feelers, and they never have legs. However, they do have a mouth opening at the front end.

Slugs and snails belong to yet another group of invertebrates.

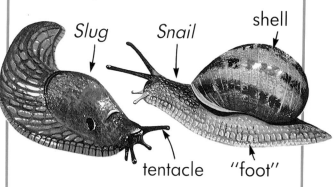

shell

Slug   *Snail*

tentacle   "foot"

They both move on a muscular "foot" and have one or two pairs of tentacles. Snails have a shell on their backs but slugs do not.

147

How invertebrates move

Many insects can fly, using one or two pairs of wings. Some can fly very fast – a Dragonfly can do 40 kilometres an hour.

A beetle has two pairs of wings.

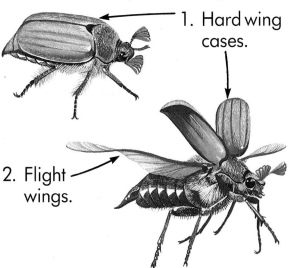

1. Hard wing cases.

2. Flight wings.

Beetles use one pair of wings in flight. They hold the wing cases out and move the flight wings up and down.

How the wings move in flight

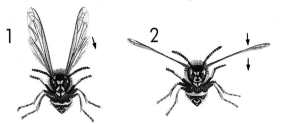

1   2

During the down stroke, the wings push the air downwards and backwards.

Bees use two pairs of wings in flight but it looks like one pair. Special hooks join the pairs of wings together.

hooks

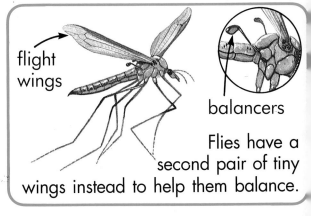

flight wings

balancers

Flies have a second pair of tiny wings instead to help them balance.

3   4

The up stroke of the wings.

Walking, jumping and crawling

This is a looper caterpillar. It brings its back legs up to the front legs and then moves the front legs forwards.

It has no legs along the middle of the body.

front legs

back legs

pads

hooks

A fly has suction pads and hooks on its feet. It can use them to walk upside down.

long, strong back legs

A grasshopper can jump 20 times the length of its own body. With its wings out, it can glide even further.

Most caterpillars have a pair of legs on most of their body segments. They move each pair a little in turn.

The front end is moving forwards.

Bristles stop the worm slipping.

An Earthworm crawls along by using its muscles to make parts of its body longer and thinner and then shorter and fatter.

How invertebrates feed

There are thousands of different invertebrates. They do not all find food or eat in the same way. Some eat plants, others eat animals or both animals and plants. A few invertebrates feed on blood.

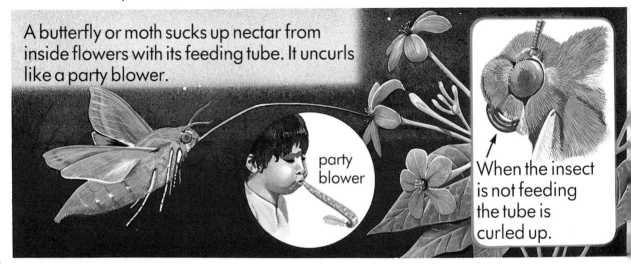

A butterfly or moth sucks up nectar from inside flowers with its feeding tube. It uncurls like a party blower.

party blower

When the insect is not feeding the tube is curled up.

pliers

A grasshopper's jaws work like a pair of pliers, nipping off bits of grass.

syringe

A female mosquito pierces the skin and sucks up blood, like a syringe.

sponge

The mouthparts of a fly soak up juices like a sponge mops up water.

Tarantula

eyes

All spiders have eight legs.

Poison from the fangs paralyses the victim. Then the spider sucks the insides dry.

snake

These are not legs, but special feelers called palps. They are like the antennae of insects.

This hairy Tarantula is a giant spider. It lives in hot countries of America. It captures small mammals, insects and small snakes.

file

Burying Beetle

This beetle is digging soil from under the dead bird, so it is slowly buried.

A snail's tongue is like a rough file. It feeds on leaves, fruit and flowers.

Burying Beetles feed on dead animals they find. The females also lay their eggs on the body once it is buried. The young feed on the body when they hatch.

151

Colours and chemicals

Many invertebrates match the colour or the shape of their surroundings.
They are camouflaged. If they keep still, they are difficult to see.
Some invertebrates have bright colours to warn enemies not to touch.
Others squirt harmful chemicals at their enemies.

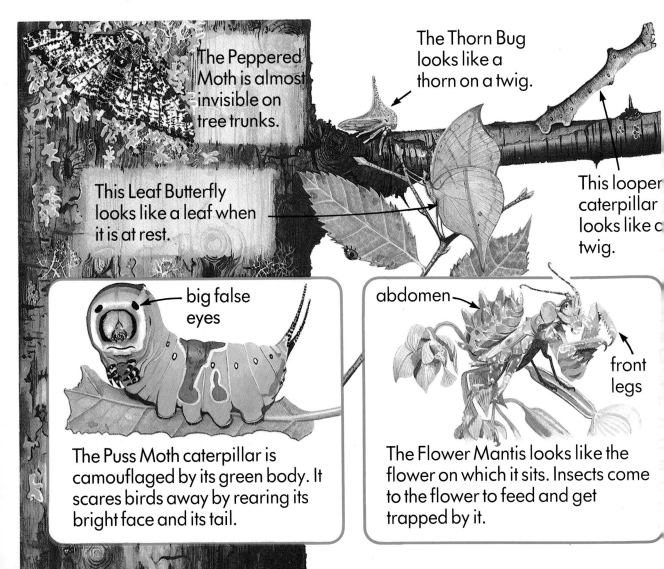

The Peppered Moth is almost invisible on tree trunks.

The Thorn Bug looks like a thorn on a twig.

This Leaf Butterfly looks like a leaf when it is at rest.

This looper caterpillar looks like a twig.

big false eyes

abdomen

front legs

The Puss Moth caterpillar is camouflaged by its green body. It scares birds away by rearing its bright face and its tail.

The Flower Mantis looks like the flower on which it sits. Insects come to the flower to feed and get trapped by it.

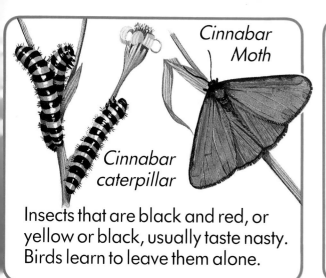

Cinnabar Moth

Cinnabar caterpillar

Insects that are black and red, or yellow or black, usually taste nasty. Birds learn to leave them alone.

acid

This Wood Ant is ready for battle. In this position it can squirt acid at enemies that come too near.

If it is startled, the Bombardier Beetle fires a gas from its rear end that irritates the eyes of the enemy. The gas pops and also forms a smoke-screen. The beetle escapes while the enemy is confused. This drives off most enemies from ants, spiders and beetles to frogs and toads.

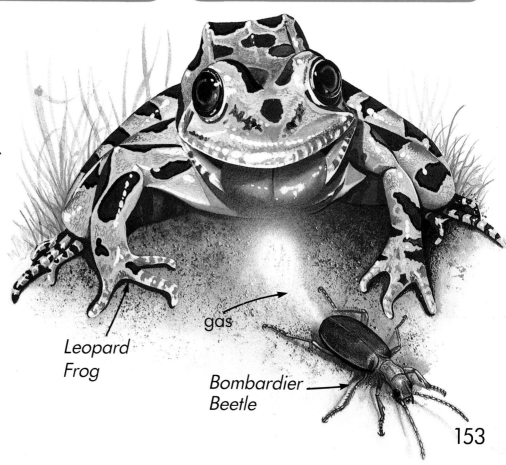

Leopard Frog

gas

Bombardier Beetle

153

Eggs and young

Most female invertebrates lay eggs. These are usually quite small. The eggs are laid alone or in groups, in different places. Usually each egg is put where there is food for the young when it hatches. You may be able to find some eggs if you look at leaves or grasses.

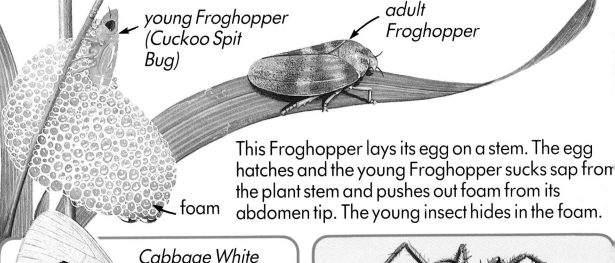

young Froghopper (Cuckoo Spit Bug)

adult Froghopper

foam

This Froghopper lays its egg on a stem. The egg hatches and the young Froghopper sucks sap from the plant stem and pushes out foam from its abdomen tip. The young insect hides in the foam.

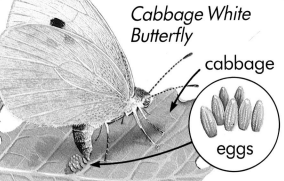

Cabbage White Butterfly

cabbage

eggs

A female butterfly lays her eggs on a leaf. The caterpillars hatch and feed on it. She flies off and does not look after her eggs or young.

Wolf Spider

Eggs in silk cocoon.

This female Wolf Spider spins a silk cocoon for her eggs. She carries it in her jaws until the eggs hatch.

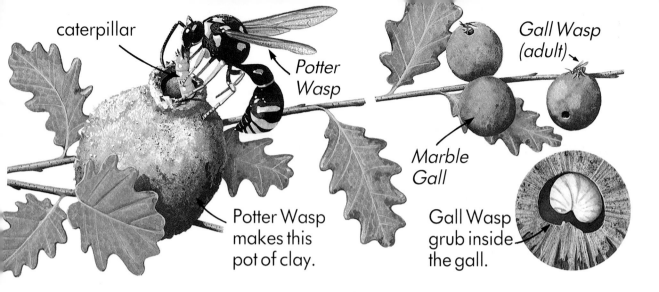

caterpillar

Potter Wasp

Potter Wasp makes this pot of clay.

Gall Wasp (adult)

Marble Gall

Gall Wasp grub inside the gall.

The Potter Wasp catches and paralyzes caterpillars. Then she pushes them into her clay pot. When it is full, she lays an egg inside. When the wasp grub hatches, it feeds on the caterpillars.

A Marble Gall is caused by a wasp that lays its egg in the bud of an oak. The oak swells around the grub and forms a gall. The wasp grub feeds on the gall until it changes into an adult wasp.

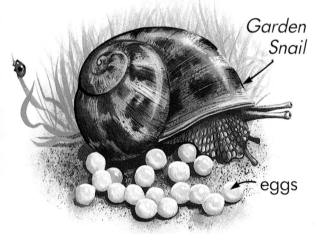

Garden Snail

eggs

A snail lays lots of eggs in the soil, then leaves them to hatch by themselves. The young look like very tiny snails.

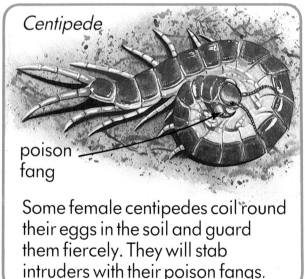

Centipede

poison fang

Some female centipedes coil round their eggs in the soil and guard them fiercely. They will stab intruders with their poison fangs.

Growing up

When a young invertebrate hatches, it often looks different from its parents. The young changes its appearance at least once before it becomes an adult. Some young invertebrates look like their parents when they are born or when they hatch.

adult

baby

Greenfly

1. Eggs   2. Young

Some Greenfly do not lay eggs at all. They can give birth to babies without mating. The babies are tiny versions of the mother.

Female snails lay eggs. When the young hatch out, they look like very tiny adults. Their shells grow as the snails get bigger.

Locust

1. Egg   eggs

wing bud

2. Nymph

wings

3. Adult

A female locust lays her eggs in damp, warm soil and leaves them to hatch.

The young looks like an adult locust but has no wings, only wing buds.

The nymph grows and changes into an adult. The adult has wings.

156

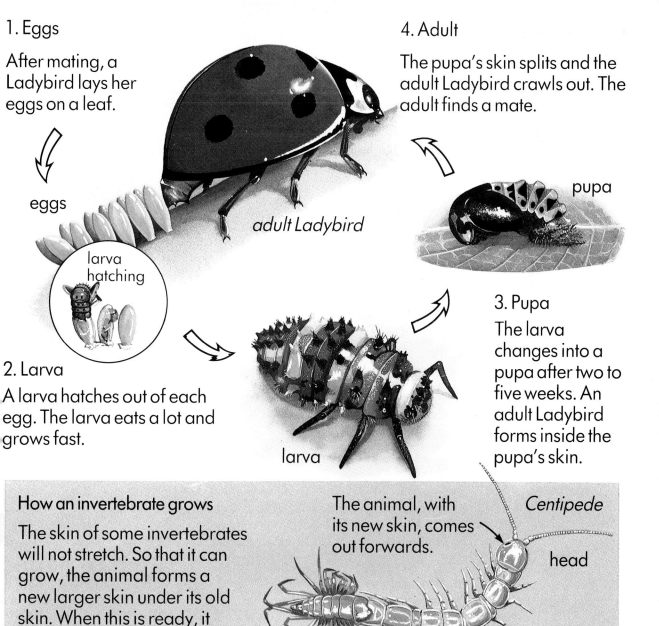

1. Eggs

After mating, a Ladybird lays her eggs on a leaf.

eggs

larva hatching

adult Ladybird

2. Larva

A larva hatches out of each egg. The larva eats a lot and grows fast.

larva

4. Adult

The pupa's skin splits and the adult Ladybird crawls out. The adult finds a mate.

pupa

3. Pupa

The larva changes into a pupa after two to five weeks. An adult Ladybird forms inside the pupa's skin.

How an invertebrate grows

The skin of some invertebrates will not stretch. So that it can grow, the animal forms a new larger skin under its old skin. When this is ready, it splits open the old skin near the head and wriggles out.

The animal, with its new skin, comes out forwards.

Centipede

head

The old skin is left behind.

157

Spiders

Spiders live in many different places. Some live in our own homes and gardens. Others live on mountains or in deserts. Most of the 60,000 different kinds of spiders are very useful to us. They eat lots of flies and other pests. All spiders have eight legs and can spin silk.

Silk is made by special organs in the abdomen.

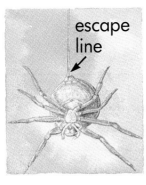

escape line

This spider spins a silk thread as an escape line.

This spider wraps its prey in silken threads.

cocoon

Spiders spin a silk cocoon to protect their eggs.

web

An Orb Spider waits for its prey to become trapped in its web. The spider does not get stuck on its own web because it has oil on its feet.

This tiny Crab Spider looks like the flower it sits on. It waits in ambush for passing insects such as bees, then grabs one in its fangs.

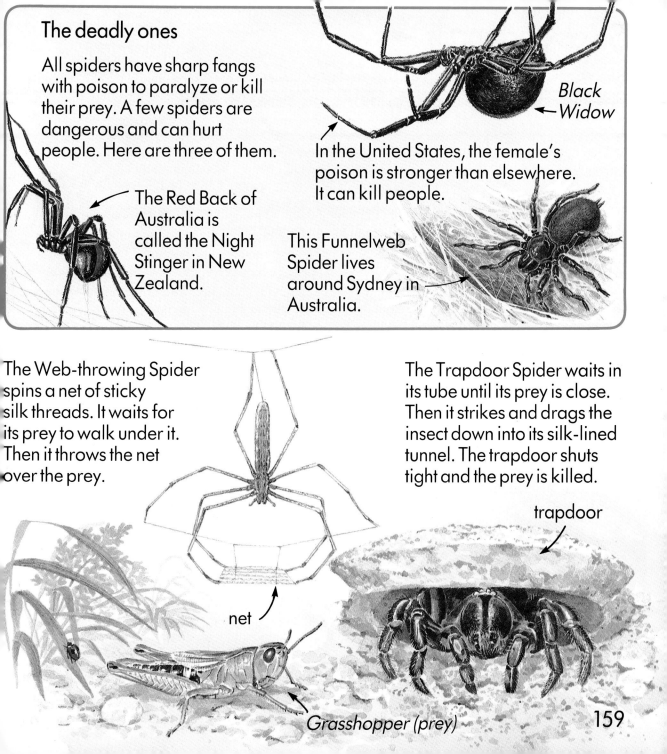

The deadly ones

All spiders have sharp fangs with poison to paralyze or kill their prey. A few spiders are dangerous and can hurt people. Here are three of them.

Black Widow

In the United States, the female's poison is stronger than elsewhere. It can kill people.

The Red Back of Australia is called the Night Stinger in New Zealand.

This Funnelweb Spider lives around Sydney in Australia.

The Web-throwing Spider spins a net of sticky silk threads. It waits for its prey to walk under it. Then it throws the net over the prey.

The Trapdoor Spider waits in its tube until its prey is close. Then it strikes and drags the insect down into its silk-lined tunnel. The trapdoor shuts tight and the prey is killed.

trapdoor

net

Grasshopper (prey)

159

Slugs and snails

Slugs and snails belong to the group called gastropods. This means "bellyfoots". Slugs are land snails that have no shell.

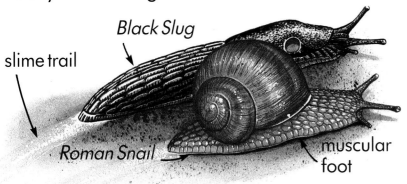

Black Slug

slime trail

Roman Snail

muscular foot

Red Slug

A slug's slime is so protective that it can climb over a very sharp knife unharmed.

Slugs and snails make a slimy substance that helps them move along. They leave a slime trail. The flat underpart of their body is called a muscular foot.

Great Grey Slug

Pointed Snail

Garden Snails

plug

Slugs and snails live in damp places among plants, under stones, or in the soil.

Banded Snail

When the weather is very dry or cold, the snail pulls its body inside its shell. Its slime hardens and forms a plug so that the snail is sealed inside. When the weather improves the plug softens.

160

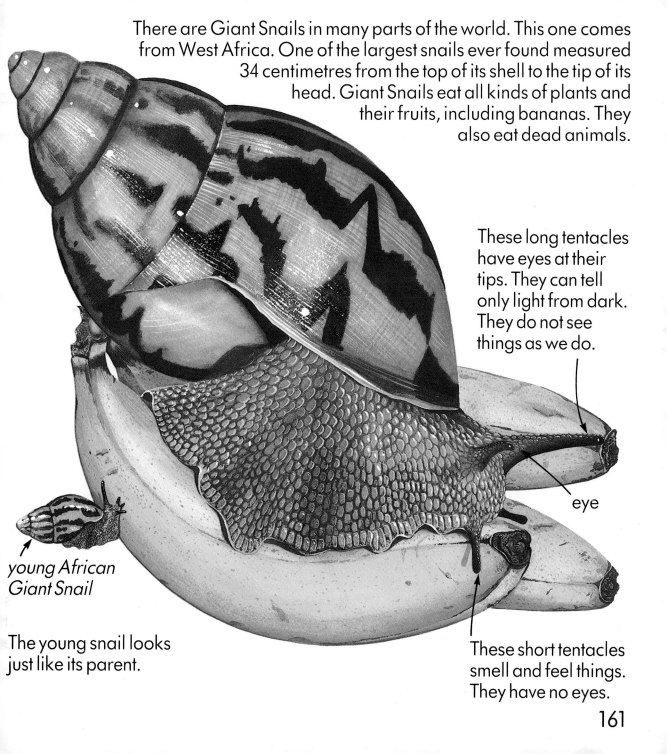

There are Giant Snails in many parts of the world. This one comes from West Africa. One of the largest snails ever found measured 34 centimetres from the top of its shell to the tip of its head. Giant Snails eat all kinds of plants and their fruits, including bananas. They also eat dead animals.

These long tentacles have eyes at their tips. They can tell only light from dark. They do not see things as we do.

eye

young African Giant Snail

The young snail looks just like its parent.

These short tentacles smell and feel things. They have no eyes.

Beetles

There are over 250,000 different kinds of beetles. Turn over a log in a forest or disturb some fallen leaves. You are likely to find a beetle.

Most beetles are quite small. A few grow to the size of these two beetles. They are drawn life size.

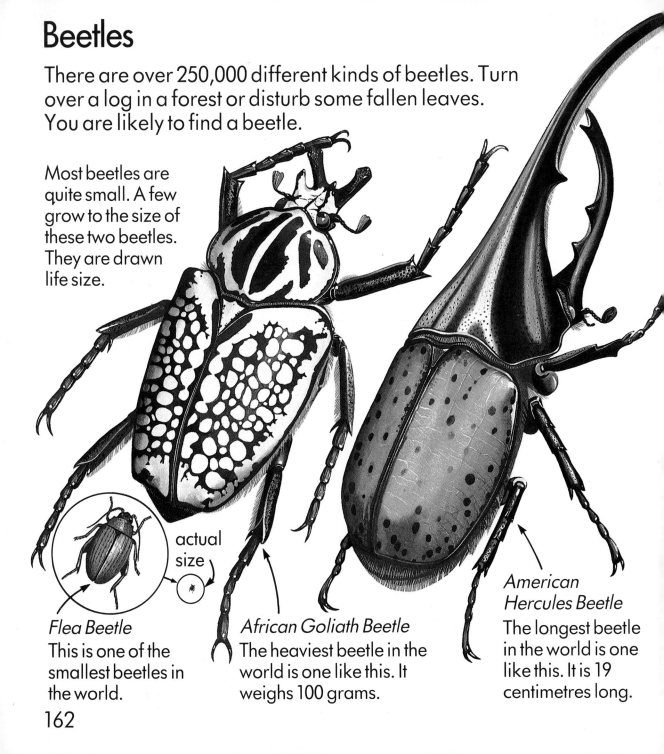

actual size

Flea Beetle
This is one of the smallest beetles in the world.

African Goliath Beetle
The heaviest beetle in the world is one like this. It weighs 100 grams.

American Hercules Beetle
The longest beetle in the world is one like this. It is 19 centimetres long.

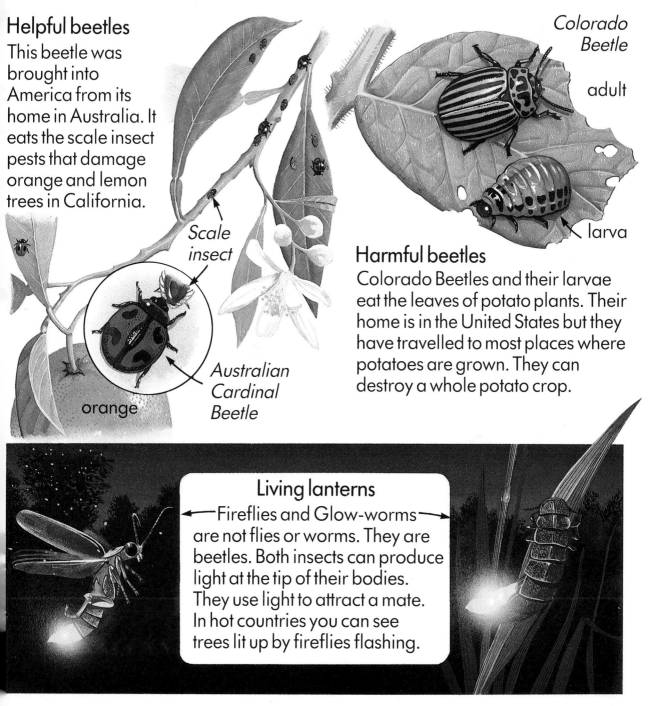

Helpful beetles

This beetle was brought into America from its home in Australia. It eats the scale insect pests that damage orange and lemon trees in California.

Scale insect

Australian Cardinal Beetle

orange

Colorado Beetle

adult

larva

Harmful beetles

Colorado Beetles and their larvae eat the leaves of potato plants. Their home is in the United States but they have travelled to most places where potatoes are grown. They can destroy a whole potato crop.

Living lanterns

Fireflies and Glow-worms are not flies or worms. They are beetles. Both insects can produce light at the tip of their bodies. They use light to attract a mate. In hot countries you can see trees lit up by fireflies flashing.

Termite cities

Some insects live and work together in large family groups. They are called social insects. Termites, ants, and some bees and wasps are social insects. Some termites build huge mounds or nests. Most termites live in hot countries and feed on wood.

Jungle termite nests

A new roof is added each year.

Termite nest cut in half to show passages inside.

worker   soldier

There are thousands of termites in each nest. These are workers and soldiers.

In tropical rain forests, where it rains a lot, termites build their nests with a roof. This works like an umbrella. It keeps heavy rain from damaging the nest.

Tree termite nest

In tropical America some termites buil their nests in trees. This Tree Ant-eate is eating the termites. It has a long, sticky tongue

The queen lays eggs. The king fertilizes them.

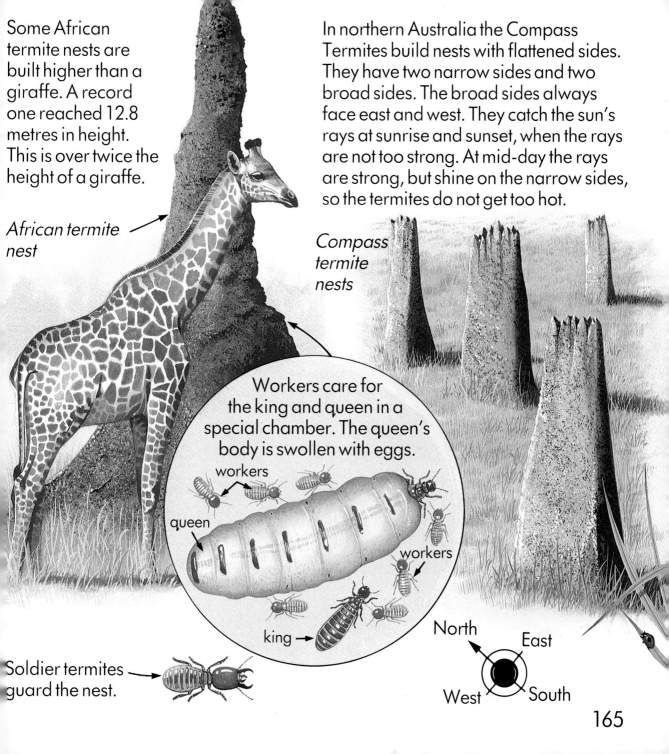

Some African termite nests are built higher than a giraffe. A record one reached 12.8 metres in height. This is over twice the height of a giraffe.

African termite nest

In northern Australia the Compass Termites build nests with flattened sides. They have two narrow sides and two broad sides. The broad sides always face east and west. They catch the sun's rays at sunrise and sunset, when the rays are not too strong. At mid-day the rays are strong, but shine on the narrow sides, so the termites do not get too hot.

Compass termite nests

Workers care for the king and queen in a special chamber. The queen's body is swollen with eggs.

workers

queen

workers

king

Soldier termites guard the nest.

North

East

West

South

165

Amazing creepy crawlies

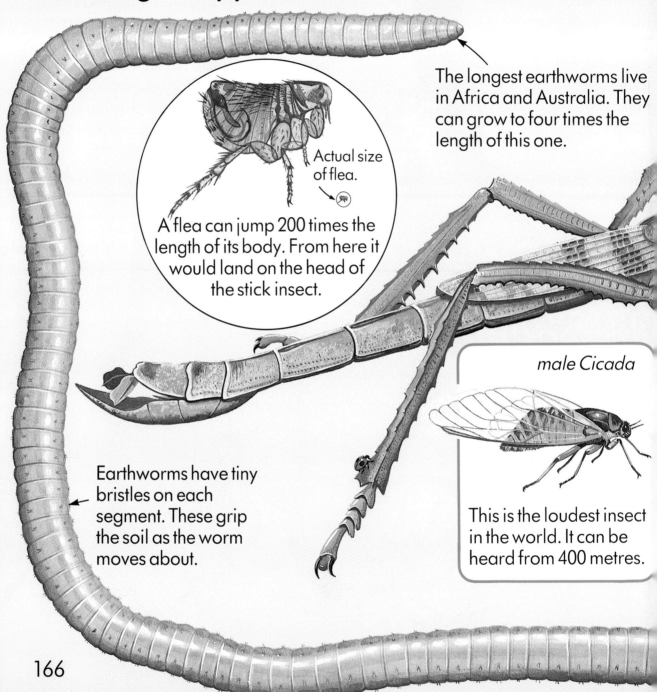

The longest earthworms live in Africa and Australia. They can grow to four times the length of this one.

Actual size of flea.

A flea can jump 200 times the length of its body. From here it would land on the head of the stick insect.

Earthworms have tiny bristles on each segment. These grip the soil as the worm moves about.

male Cicada

This is the loudest insect in the world. It can be heard from 400 metres.

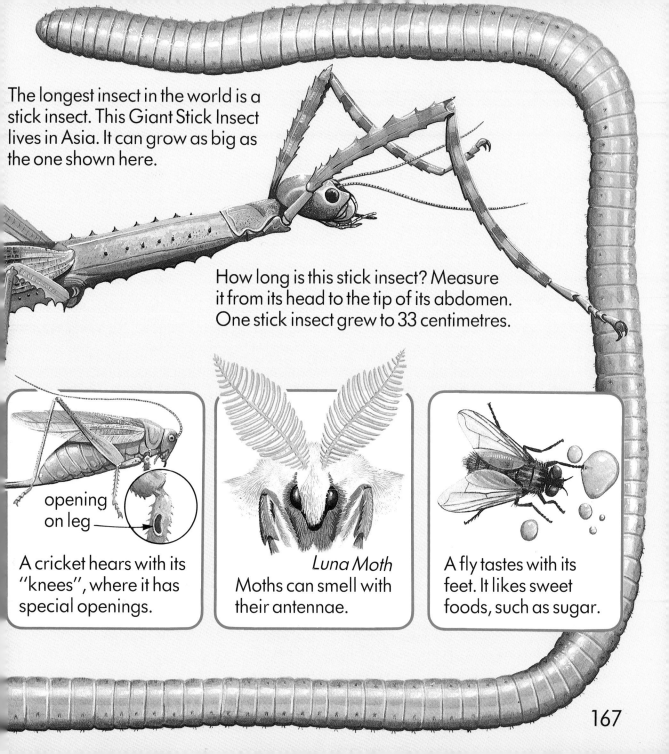

The longest insect in the world is a stick insect. This Giant Stick Insect lives in Asia. It can grow as big as the one shown here.

How long is this stick insect? Measure it from its head to the tip of its abdomen. One stick insect grew to 33 centimetres.

opening on leg

A cricket hears with its "knees", where it has special openings.

Luna Moth
Moths can smell with their antennae.

A fly tastes with its feet. It likes sweet foods, such as sugar.